TOM WEDGWOOD
AT
WATERLOO

TOM WEDGWOOD
AT
WATERLOO

THE LIFE OF THOMAS JOSIAH WEDGWOOD
A SOLDIER WHO FOUGHT AT WATERLOO

ANTONY WEDGWOOD

UNICORN

First published by Unicorn
an imprint of the Unicorn Publishing Group LLP, 2018
5 Newburgh Street
London W1F 7RG

www.unicornpublishing.org

10 9 8 7 6 5 4 3 2 1

ISBN 978-1-911604-95-2

Printed in India

On the day after the Battle of Waterloo, Ensign Thomas Josiah Wedgwood, 3rd Foot Guards, wrote to his mother:

The right wing of our regiment and my company went to the assistance of the Coldstreams in the wood.

The picture on the front cover is by Denis Dighton, based on sketches that he made on the actual battlefield only a few days after the event. It shows the struggle that Tom describes outside the bitterly contested Chateau of Hougoumont.

CONTENTS

FOREWORD

As a seventeen-year-old Ensign in the 3rd Foot Guards, Thomas Josiah Wedgwood fought at Waterloo and took part in the crucial defence of Hougoumont. He left no descendants to remember him in future generations, but a hundred years later three letters that he wrote immediately after the battle were published in *A Century of Family Letters*. It is largely for this that he is known today.

Tom's career started dramatically: what happened to him afterwards was almost inevitably an anti-climax. However, he lived through particularly interesting times and I thought that a more rounded account of his life could usefully contribute to what was already familiar. Some periods are rather sparsely documented but I hope that I have managed to do him justice.

In order to put his Waterloo letters into context I have included a certain amount about the battle and the events leading up to it. However, there is no point in writing yet another history of Waterloo, which has been done many times by those who are far more expert than me. For a deeper understanding, the more recent works tend to be the best researched and those listed in the bibliography are very readable.

Almost nothing would have been possible without the tremendous help and support that I have received from the Wedgwood Museum, and in particular from their Curator, Gaye Blake-Roberts, and their Archivist, Lucy Lead, who have been unfailingly helpful and have provided much of the basis of this work. I am also indebted to Peter Hyland, whose shrewd and impartial comments on the final draft were more than welcome. Finally, I must mention the London Library in St James's Square, which has made the process of digging into obscure corners of the early nineteenth century an enormous and instructive pleasure.

Antony Wedgwood
2018

TOM'S FAMILY BACKGROUND

JOHN AND JENNY WEDGWOOD

In August 1792, Josiah Wedgwood II and his sister Susannah, offspring of the great Josiah, visited Pembrokeshire for the balls and races that took place during the Haverfordwest Assizes. Jos* took an immediate liking to Bessy Allen, the daughter of John Bartlett Allen of Cresselly: the feeling was mutual and by Christmas they were married. Two years later, Jos's older brother John succumbed to the charms of her sister, Louisa Jane, always known as Jane or Jenny.

Both John and Jenny came from large families, as was normal in those times. The Wedgwoods were extremely wealthy – nouveaux riches in fact – and the Allens were country gentry, deriving their money largely from coal; but the Wedgwoods had benefitted from a wide education that did not stop at formal schooling, whereas the Allens appear to have been rather conventional in their outlook.

To an extent, perhaps, John had something of his father's enquiring mind, but he was entirely lacking in determination and could not bring himself to take a serious interest in the pottery works. Instead, he bought himself a partnership in a bank, which frequently went through difficulties and finally collapsed in 1816: John was always incapable of managing money and had to be rescued by a family subscription. His real interest, however, was horticulture and he can claim to be a founder of the Royal Horticultural Society – or even the founder, since

---

* The family has often been rather unoriginal in its choice of names: Josiah, Thomas, John, Sarah, Elizabeth and their diminutives recur in almost every generation. Josiah II is referred to in this work as Jos – which most of the Josiahs were called, at least when they were grown-up.

John Wedgwood

it was at his suggestion that the first meeting of its promoters was held, and he chaired that meeting himself.

The Allen sisters were less fortunate in their education and suffered from having a rather disagreeable and morose father. Despite this disadvantage – or perhaps because of it – they had charming personalities and were excellent conversationalists. They were also superb letter-writers, whose affection and empathy shine through their correspondence.

Jenny Allen

Henrietta Litchfield wrote in *A Century of Family Letters:*

Louisa Jane Allen ... was the beauty of the family. Bessy spoke of her incomparable cheerfulness, and said: 'With her the sun always shines, and she seems to trip rather than slide down the hill of life.' My mother [Emma Darwin] told us that the warmth and graciousness of her aunt Jane's welcome was quite unique in its charm.[1]

Jenny needed to be cheerful, as her life was perennially clouded by John's financial difficulties and worries about their children's health. Of their seven children, Eliza, Allen and Caroline were her chief concern.* Caroline died in 1825; Eliza and Allen lived for many years thereafter. Exactly what was wrong with them is not always clear; 'consumption' (or tuberculosis) is often mentioned. It was certainly a major killer in those days, but the diagnosis might be questioned in one or two cases, especially Allen's, whose perpetual invalidism looks suspiciously like extreme and rather self-centred hypochondria.

Whatever the cause or causes, but quite possibly in consequence of the results, Jenny became seriously religious in her later life and moved towards the Evangelicals, which rather puzzled the more broadminded Jos Wedgwoods. Henrietta Litchfield ascribes this mainly to the influence of Dr John Baron, who treated Jenny's children,[2] but her sister Caroline Drewe was another possible source, favoured by Barbara and Hensleigh Wedgwood in *The Wedgwood Circle, 1730–1897*. Caroline had been left on her own when her husband died in 1810, and this was followed over the next few years by the deaths of three of their children which, as an 'Advanced Christian', she accepted as God's divine will.[3]

Quite where John stood on this religiosity, we do not really know. His parents had been Unitarian, although this began to fade with passing generations and most of the Wedgwoods eventually came to some sort of accommodation with more moderate Anglicanism. It may however explain why two of his four sons went into the church, which was otherwise an unusual career choice for the family.

---

* For a more detailed account of the various family members and relationships, which can be quite complicated, see the Biographical Notes in Appendix I.

THEIR SON, THOMAS JOSIAH WEDGWOOD

Thomas Josiah Wedgwood was the John Wedgwoods' third child and second son, born in 1797 at Cote House, Westbury-on-Trym, where they had recently settled.

Cote House in about 1791, from a watercolour by Turner

We know little of Tom's early years, apart from the fact that he was educated for a brief period at Westminster School, followed by a year at Sandhurst and after that perhaps some private tuition on subjects important for a military career.[4] In January 1814 he was commissioned as an Ensign into the 3rd Foot Guards – now known as the Scots Guards.

At that point Napoleon was still in power but it seems very unlikely that Tom was involved in the tail end of the campaign against him; Paris surrendered to the forces of the Sixth Coalition at the end of March and it then took less than a month for Napoleon to be deposed and exiled to Elba.

Our first clear sighting of Tom is in Belgium, towards the end of that year.

PRELUDE TO BATTLE

BELGIUM

For the previous twenty years Belgium had been treated simply as a part of France, and for almost 200 years before then it had been subject to the Austrian Emperor. The victorious Allies initially returned it to Austrian rule, but shortly afterwards changed their minds. Together with the United Provinces (which were essentially modern Holland), Belgium became part of a new kingdom. It was to be ruled by the House of Orange and known as The United Kingdom of the Netherlands.

In the aftermath of French occupation, the administrative structure of Belgium was weak, but there was a small British force in the United Provinces that was moved southwards to ensure stability while the Congress of Vienna hammered out the future shape of Europe. In August 1814 Tom's battalion, previously just inside Holland at Steenbergen, was posted to Brussels and Tom became part of the British garrison.[5]

For decades France and its northern neighbours had been closed to British visitors, but once opened up by Napoleon's defeat, Belgium – and in particular Brussels – became a popular destination. By the end of the year it was home to a large British community who kept themselves amused with balls, dinner parties, picnics and horse races – and, needless to say, the presence of so many unattached young officers made for an ideal marriage market.

There was a mild panic at the end of February 1815 when Napoleon escaped from Elba and arrived in Paris, but two weeks later the Congress of Vienna declared him an outlaw – effectively a declaration of war against Napoleon himself, rather than against France – and formed the Seventh Coalition, comprising Britain, Russia, Prussia,

Sweden, Austria, the Netherlands and various German states. The Foot Guards marched off towards the frontier and Tom left the metropolitan delights of Brussels for less exciting quarters near Enghien, about 20 miles to the southwest. Civilian life went back, more or less, to what had come to be regarded as normal.

However, it was obvious that Napoleon, now re-established in power, would move against the Coalition: the question was when and where.

THE ARMIES OF THE SEVENTH COALITION

Each of the Great Powers – Britain, Austria, Russia and Prussia – had pledged an army of 150,000 men. The British and Prussians were the first to organise themselves and established bases in Belgium, preparatory to an invasion of France. Napoleon had to defeat their forces before the other powers could arrive on the scene.

The British Army had never been on the scale of the Continental ones. Furthermore, much of it was still overseas and even in those days the idea of a 'peace dividend' was politically attractive. Britain was thus unable to meet this military commitment on her own and supplemented it by paying subsidies to other states, who provided additional troops under Wellington's overall command. The result was that almost two thirds of the 73,000 men who fought under him at Waterloo were not British.[6]

Of these a very large element spoke German as their first language. About 7,000 were from the King's German Legion, a British army unit made up of expatriate Hanoverians that had been formed after Napoleon had invaded and dissolved the Electorate; they had a particular score to settle and fought with great distinction at Waterloo. There were also 12,000 more from Hanover, 7,000 from Nassau and 6,000 from Brunswick; the Nassauers and Brunswickers, in particular, were very inexperienced.

Finally, there were about 10,000 Dutch and 4,000 Belgians. The Belgian element was especially problematic, as it included both Flemish and French speakers. There is also some suggestion that having recently been part of France and being directly in the path of any future French invasion, these troops might have had divided loyalties, or were at least prepared to hedge their bets: some of them had actually fought against the British in previous campaigns. The same could be said, but to a lesser degree, in the case of certain Dutch and even Nassau troops. Whether or not wholly justified, such thoughts were clearly present in the minds of the British and perhaps account for some of Tom's less charitable remarks about the Belgians.

AWAITING NAPOLEON: THE ANGLO-ALLIED AND PRUSSIAN DISPOSITIONS

Wellington's headquarters were based in Brussels, where he also kept his reserves. The main part of the Anglo-Allied army was cantoned in three groups to the south and west, roughly along an arc about 15–20 miles from Brussels. Estimates of the total number of troops at Wellington's disposal vary, but about 110,000 might be a reasonable figure. The Prussian army of about 130,000 men under Field Marshal von Blücher was similarly distributed to the southeast, with their headquarters at Namur. The overall purpose was to provide a defensive screen around Brussels, and to protect the British lines of communication to the west and the Prussian lines to the east: end to end, the forward perimeter was about 120 miles long. The hope was that Napoleon would make his intentions clear in time for the allies to concentrate their forces. This was never going to be easy, as we shall see. This factor, and the need to keep some troops to guard the lines of potential retreat, account for most of the difference between the numbers theoretically available and those who actually fought at Waterloo.

To make sense of what follows, it is also necessary to understand a little about the structure of the British army (a more comprehensive description is given in Appendix IV).

For the infantry, the basic tactical unit was the battalion: a regiment could have several battalions, but it was essentially an administrative body. Higher formations were made up of battalions from various regiments, but not necessarily all the battalions of the same regiment. Tom was in the 2nd Battalion of the 3rd Foot Guards, which would nowadays (and perhaps rather curiously) be abbreviated to the 2/3rd Foot Guards. A typical Guards battalion numbered about 1,000 men, on the high side for the army as a whole. It was divided into ten companies of roughly equal size; Tom was in the 5th Company of his battalion, commanded by Captain & Lieutenant Colonel* Canning, but since Canning was acting as one of Wellington's ADCs, the actual role fell to Lieutenant & Captain Edward Fairfield.

Tom Wedgwood to his sister Caroline – 7 June 1815

The first known letter from Tom was written to his sister Caroline on 7 June. By that time, he was encamped at Hérinnes (now better known by its Flemish name Herne), just north of the Guards' Divisional Headquarters at Enghien. Caroline was almost exactly sixteen at the time, and much of the letter is filled with the sort of domestic detail that a brother might write to a slightly younger sister. However, it also shows that militarily, things were coming to a head. Although neither of them could know it, Waterloo was less than two weeks away.

---

* This is an example of the 'double ranking' system then used in the Guards. As far as his role in the battalion was concerned, he was the equivalent of a Captain, but in order to retain precedence above the other regiments, he was also given the army rank of Lieutenant Colonel. In his letters, Tom uses the higher ranks.

Hérinnes
June 7ᵗʰ 1815

My dear Caroline

I believe you are next on my roster, for a letter which I must say you deserve more than any of them. I have just this moment received Charles's letter and it being a dreadful rainy day I lose no time in answering it. Pray congratulate him on my part for his being at last appointed, to take his examination for Woolwich for the success of which my most hearty wishes will accompany him.

Charles was their younger brother and reputed to be 'an undisciplined and adventurous young man'.[7] He was clearly contemplating an army career, although the reference to Woolwich is a bit puzzling as he eventually became a Lieutenant in the East India Company's service; Woolwich was the college which prospective gunners and sappers in the British army would attend, and the East India Company had recently established its own college at Addiscombe.

Tom then describes what has been going on with his regiment. As a very junior officer, preparations for active service seem to have largely taken the form of reviews.

We have remained here very quietly ever since I wrote last, but we expect to move almost immediately. Last Tuesday* week there was a review of all the British cavalry out here, by the Duke of Wellington and Marshal Blucher which without exception was the finest sight I ever saw. There were 46 squadrons of cavalry and 8 troops of horse artillery, the finest I suppose in the world. The review was near Grammont about 3 leagues from here in

---

* The review was actually held on 29 May, which was a Monday rather than a Tuesday.

a large meadow for the use of which Lord Uxbridge paid 200
guineas. It lasted about 4 hours. There was an immense crowd
there both of English and Flemish as well as Germans, Prussian,
Russian &c &c. These were very much astonished at the beauty
of our horses and the appearance of the troops altogether.

The story of how much Uxbridge had paid to hire the meadow lost nothing in its telling. According to Captain Mercer, who commanded G Troop Royal Horse Artillery during the Battle of Waterloo, it was said that 'as much as £400 or £500 were paid'.[8]

Tom does not mention this, but Mercer also relates that in the lead-up to the cavalry review, the duc de Berry had turned up, expecting to be given a general salute; his father was heir to the French throne and he was in command of the royalist French army, but had fled to Ghent. The troopers were busy grooming their horses and generally making themselves look respectable, and were somewhat disconcerted to hear cries of 'The Duke – the Duke's coming', assuming that they meant the Duke of Wellington. The panic passed and they got back to their grooming as soon as they discovered that it was only the duc de Berry; when Wellington arrived his reception was somewhat different. Uxbridge later excused himself by saying that he had had no instructions on the matter.

Another review took place a few days later, this time by the Prince of Orange. It was less well received, partly because of the bad weather and partly because the Prince's enthusiasm for parades and drills was not always shared by the troops.*

---

* The plain on which the review took place was probably the Heath of Casteau, about halfway between Soignies and Mons. Tom's sentiments about the review were widely shared and are frequently mentioned by other contemporary sources. See, for example, *The Journals of the Late Major MacReady – United Service Magazine*: July 1852, p. 343.

On Thursday* our division was reviewed by the Prince of Orange. We marched on Wednesday from here and were quartered in some villages in the neighbourhood of Mons about 5 leagues from here. Next morning we marched about 2 leagues further to a large plain, had a long review and marched back to our quarters & next day returned here. It was very unfortunate that there was rain for almost the whole of the 3 days so that we were well soaked each day and having to sleep on straw and the greatest difficulty to get anything to eat, I did not find the excursion very agreeable. However the Prince was very well pleased and praised us very much.

Tom then reverts to family matters. At the time, Allen was a bit of a worry to his parents, who thought him so withdrawn that they were concerned about his mental stability. He was sent abroad to find his feet and seems to have been in Holland at this point.[9]

I received a letter from Allen a few days ago. He sent me a letter to a family at Ath which he had got through the means of Mr Barensfeldt thinking I was at that place. I do not know the reason that I am always told to write to some particular one among you, I suppose that my letters are seen by the whole family and therefore cannot make much difference. You see that I humour you young ones and that is the reason I do not write so often to my father and mother because I imagine they have too much sense to mind who the letter is directed to. Bye the bye I suppose it is for much the same reason that I get so few letters from them. Charles's letter was not very satisfactory, he does not tell me how my mother is but fills his letter about fishing, flies, floats &c.

---

* Again, Tom seems to have got his days of the week wrong. The review took place on Wednesday 31 May (*Hamilton*, p. 13).

The introduction obtained by Allen was probably never used, as Ath is about 15 miles away from where Tom was stationed and, given the state of things, he was unlikely to have had much free time. It has proved impossible to trace the Mr Barensfeldt who provided it, although he may have been a correspondent of Davison's bank, in which John was a partner: a banker named Barensfeld (sic) is listed as trading in Amsterdam during that period. However, Coutts, which took over Davison's when it collapsed the following year, can find nothing in their archives.*

I am sorry to hear that Scarlet Fever is in the family especially as it seems likely to hinder your receiving a very pleasant visit. It is now a long time since I have seen any of my friends in England, a much longer space than I have ever before passed without seeing some of them and I often feel a longing after old England but it would be a great deal that would tempt me to go there if it was in my power.

A terrible misfortune happened to me yesterday. I had been dining at Enghien yesterday and riding home again my horse ran a nail into his foot which I pulled out. He went a little lame with it at first but he seemed quite well before I got home and I thought nothing of it but my servant has just told me that he is so lame in that foot that he can hardly put it on the ground. I have sent for a farrier to put something on it but I am afraid it will be sometime before it gets quite well.

---

* The bank was known officially by various names, the changes reflecting changes in the partnership and usually another injection of capital. It is often referred to as Davison's, after Alexander Davison – a British Government contractor of uncertain reputation – who rescued it in 1803, and sometimes as the London & Middlesex Bank. As with many bank failures, the partners seem to have over extended themselves and forgotten what banking was about.

It has to be said that Tom's idea of a 'terrible misfortune' seems trivial compared with what was to come.

Tell Charles if this letter arrives in time that when he goes to Woolwich for his examination that he must have great confidence in himself, must not be at all in a fright or flurried but must be cool, if he is asked questions he must take time and consider before he answers them and not to be in too great a hurry and then he may depend upon his passing. I believe that half the people who do not pass examinations do badly on account of their being in a fright and not because they are deficient in what they are examined in. I have myself been examined several times and know what it is you must do. Tell him to write to me directly he goes there that I may know the proper method of directing to him and that I mean we should keep up a sharp correspondence.

When I hear next I hope there may be nothing about the Scarlet Fever. There was something in Charles's letter about John Abbot which I could not read owing [to] having put it in a little corner in which there was not room. I shall expect to hear something soon about the things I desired to be sent to me. Give my best love to all friends and believe me

Yours most affectionately
T Wedgwood

I am in good health and spirits and in very good condition. All the people of this country tell me that they see very plainly that their country does not disagree with me.

'John Abbot' is most likely to be John White Abbott, a wealthy artist whose family had property in Exeter. Because of financial difficulties, the John Wedgwoods had 'downsized' from Cote House some years previously and returned to Staffordshire. However, after a few years they were on the move again and by 1812 had settled in Exeter, which was probably chosen in order to be near Jenny's widowed sister, Caroline Drewe (see above and Biographical notes in Appendix I, as Caroline Allen).

THE BATTLE OF WATERLOO

OPENING MOVES

Evening – 15 June 1815

Amongst the new residents of Brussels were the Duke and Duchess of Richmond, together with five of their seven daughters, three younger sons and nine servants, who had moved there for reasons of (relative) economy. They were top of the list in expatriate British society and the duchess had organised a ball on the evening of 15 June, eight days after Tom's first letter. It was essentially a social affair but inevitably included a very large army contingent, from the Duke of Wellington downwards. And so, while Ensign Tom Wedgwood was settling down to sleep in the field, the more senior and better connected officers were preparing themselves for the pleasure of her company.

In the late afternoon of that day, Wellington learnt that Napoleon had crossed the Franco-Belgian frontier and that initial contact had been made with the Prussians along the river Sambre. He put his forces on high alert but still allowed the ball to go ahead; amongst other things, it would have been pointless to do anything else as many of the senior officers were in transit from their commands, and it is even arguable that having them in one place for briefing might have been an advantage. However, he was still uncertain about Napoleon's intentions, and worried that he would try to envelop Brussels by pushing upwards to the west, which would disrupt the British supply lines from Ostend.

In fact, Napoleon was aiming to divide the Anglo-Allied and Prussian forces, exploiting possible weaknesses in communication between the two armies and relying on speed to prevent them massing together; his chosen route was roughly along the line due north to

Brussels. Famously, at about midnight Wellington was informed that his Netherlands troops were holding a position against the French at Quatre Bras, a strategically important crossroads where the main route north from Charleroi to Brussels intersected with the road between the Prussians to the east and the Anglo-Allies to the west. As it happens, the presence of the Netherlanders was against Wellington's orders: he had forbidden any concentration of his forces east of Nivelles, in order to guard the road from Mons to Brussels. Fortunately, the extremely competent Major General de Constant Rebecque, who was the Prince of Orange's Chief of Staff, had his doubts and these were shared by Lieutenant General de Perponcher-Sedlnitzky, Commander of the 2nd Netherlands Division. As a result, two rather inexperienced brigades under de Perponcher-Sedlnitzky's command were there to hold up the French.

The march to Quatre Bras

However, much more was needed. Wellington's staff spent the next hour or two drafting orders and settling routes – even a single battalion on the march would occupy about 300 yards of road. And as we shall see, Tom's own battalion received its orders at about 2.00 am and finally moved from camp at 5.00 am on 16 June. Whether by accident or design, his battalion had already been moved slightly further south* and was encamped at Petit-Rœulx, not far from the Headquarters of I Corps at Braine-le-Comte: this took 8 or 9 miles off the distance that they would otherwise had had to cover, but still left a considerable way to go.

---

* En route, they would have marched through Steenkirk, where an allied force was defeated by the French during the Nine Years' War against Louis XIV. We tend to remember the War of the Spanish Succession, a few years later, where the result was much more satisfactory.

At the time, the main roads – known as chaussées – were metalled but the lesser cross-country roads cannot have been much better than cart tracks. Earlier that month the highly experienced and practical Colonel Alexander Woodford, then in command of the 2/Coldstream and eventually to be a Field Marshal, had written:

At first, folks persevered in keeping carts, but only the high roads are paved, & in wet the cross roads and even the sides of the high roads are impassible. I established a regular peninsular train under General Carter* from the first & now all carts and carriages are strictly forbidden, a very proper measure, I am convinced; though many are unreasonable & stupid enough to grumble.[10]

The more detailed modern maps still identify the chaussées as such; they are usually quite straight and easy to recognise. Tom's route only picks up the chaussée as it gets towards Nivelles, about nine miles from Quatre Bras. They had started by moving to Braine-le-Comte, where the chaussée north to Brussels crosses the road from Petit-Rœulx to Nivelles. The town was seething with traffic, either taking baggage back to Brussels or – like the Guards – heading to do battle further east; adherence to the Woodford doctrine had, for once, proved impossible. Tom's battalion halted just outside Nivelles while the rest of the Guards came up from Enghien, and then the whole division passed through Nivelles and on to Quatre Bras. Tom had marched about 22 miles to the battlefield, but the others had even further to go.†
Without much sleep, with full equipment and in the heat of summer, it must have been very exhausting indeed.

---

* A name and rank probably intended humorously.
† The Scots Guards Association maintain that the march was no less than 27 miles, a figure that can be reconciled with Tom's by including the stretch from Enghien to Petit-Rœulx. For whatever reason, Tom was luckier than some of the others.

The Battle of Quatre Bras – 16 June 1815

The Anglo-Allies fed in reinforcements as soon as they arrived, and after initial reverses the battle of Quatre Bras effectively ended in a draw – but an important one that prevented Napoleon from making progress towards Brussels. Of those who arrived in time, the Guards division had furthest to come and got there in the late afternoon, when their presence helped the Allies to counter-attack and stabilise the situation. The two battalions of 1st Foot Guards went straight into action, while the Coldstreams and Tom's battalion were largely kept in reserve, although they did engage in a little skirmishing during the following morning. Whether this was because they had only recently absorbed some large drafts from the militia and were perhaps not so battle-hardened, or simply because the 1st Foot Guards led the line of march, is not entirely clear. At Waterloo itself the position was reversed, with the Coldstreams and 3rd Foot Guards – who had suffered almost no casualties at Quatre Bras – taking the brunt of the initial fighting.

That afternoon, the Prussians also met the French at Ligny, about 5 miles to the east, and did less well. Tactically, the French won the battle and inflicted considerable losses, but they failed to stop Blücher from regrouping and advancing in support of Wellington.

Withdrawal to Mont St Jean – 17 June 1815

Early the next morning the Anglo-Allied army withdrew towards Brussels and took up position on the Heights of Mont St Jean, a slight ridge about 2 miles below the actual village of Waterloo. It was an almost perfect defensive position, giving the advantage of a reverse slope behind the ridge on which the main strength of Wellington's army was placed.

Forward of the ridge there were three farm complexes: Papelotte on the extreme left of the line, La Haye Sainte roughly in the centre and Hougoumont on the right, rather closer to the French. The buildings

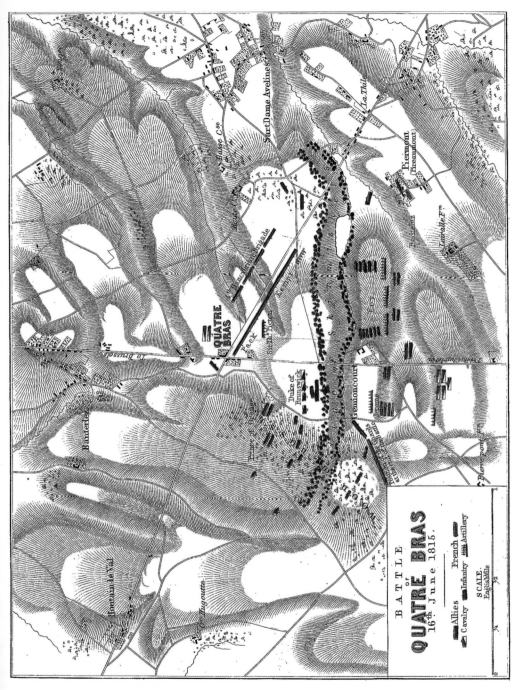

The Battle of Quatre Bras towards the end of the day. The wood which Tom
mentions in his letter (the 'Wood of Bossu' on this map) is on the right of the
Anglo-Allied line.

were fortified as strongpoints in order to break up the French advance: the British occupied Hougoumont and the King's German Legion occupied La Haye Sainte, which they were to defend tenaciously until they ran out of ammunition and were overwhelmed. Papelotte was more lightly defended, partly because it lay closest to the expected Prussian advance and partly because it was furthest away from the main French concentration.

The weather broke towards the evening and torrential rain fell all night, with significant consequences for what was to come.

HOUGOUMONT

The struggle for Hougoumont has been studied and written about almost as much as Waterloo itself and it was there that Tom took part in his first serious action.

The position included a complex of farm buildings and domestic grounds, with a formal garden and orchard. The buildings enclosed two courtyards gated to the outside world; the gardens and orchard were protected by walls. There was also a wooded area immediately facing the enemy, which would hold them up and screen the defenders from artillery fire. In short, the whole arrangement was admirable for defence.

On the evening of 17 June, the light companies of the four Guards battalions were sent into Hougoumont to prepare for battle. These were picked men trained as mobile troops and skirmishers, often brigaded together as a single fighting unit. On the following morning, two of these companies were withdrawn and replaced by relatively inexperienced Hanoverians and Nassauers: the latter, rather confusingly, were for dynastic reasons part of the Netherlands army.*

---

* Despite their inexperience and an unclear chain of command, they were to perform very well in the chaotic fighting which ensued at Hougoumont. Their leader, Captain Büsgen, deserves a great deal of credit.

The opening positions of the armies at the Battle of Waterloo.
Hougoumont, where Tom Fought, is clearly marked between
the British and French armies.

At that point, there were about 1,200 allied soldiers in and around Hougoumont, of which three-quarters were Nassauers and only 200 or so were British. The bulk of the Guards division took up position on the ridge about 400-500 yards immediately behind the farm and on the right of the Anglo-Allied army.

The main battle started at about 11.30 am when Hougoumont and its surroundings immediately came under attack; gradually, more men were fed in to its defence and others, exhausted by fighting and by losses, were replaced with fresh troops from the 2/Coldstream and Tom's battalion, the 2/3rd Guards. At the peak of the fighting perhaps 2,600 allied troops had been committed to the battle, but the effective number at various stages is not known because of casualties: in total these amounted to about one third.

In contrast, the French eventually committed 12,000 to 13,000 men to the attack.[11] Not only did they fail to capture Hougoumont, but by doing so reduced the odds against the Allies in other parts of the field.

Tom became involved between 2.00 and 2.30 pm when his company was sent down from the ridge to help the light companies of the 1st Guards, who were fighting in the orchard; apart from those two companies, the defence of that area was split roughly evenly between the 2/Coldstreams, the 2/3rd Guards and the Nassauers. The orchard was retaken and by late afternoon the fighting in and around Hougoumont became less intense, but while the Prussians were closing in on Napoleon's right, the French launched a last assault. The Guards responded with a charge and cleared them from the buildings, while a mixed bag of reinforcements from the King's German Legion, Hanoverians and Brunswickers helped to clear the orchard and wood.[12]

In the meantime, the Prussians started to arrive. The first ones visible to the British were elements of von Ziethen's I corps, who engaged the French at Papelotte, on the extreme left of Wellington's line. It had taken all the persuasive powers of Wellington's liaison officer, von

Müffling, to get von Ziethen to skirt around the village of Plancenoit, where the Prussians were already engaged on Napoleon's right flank, and to link up with Wellington. This took place at about 7.30 pm; the main body of Prussians probably arrived a little later at about 8.00 pm, having broken through at Plancenoit.*

At about 8.30 pm the French began to retreat and Wellington signalled a general advance. The Battle of Waterloo had been won.

TOM DESCRIBES THE BATTLE

Tom Wedgwood to his mother Jenny Wedgwood – 19 June 1815

The very next day, Tom wrote his first letter about the battle. By then he was at Nivelles, some 10 miles south of Waterloo: the French army had ceased to be an effective force, but it was still vital for the Allies to get to Paris as quickly as possible.

Tom's letter is a chronological description of events, starting with the order to move during the night of 15/16 June. He starts by describing the march to Quatre Bras, although he does not name it as such, and then the battle of Quatre Bras itself. After withdrawing to the Heights of Mt St Jean, they spent a miserable, rainy night before battle was joined. The main action that he relates is that of Hougoumont.

Brief biographical details of the officers named by Tom are given in Appendix II. Two of those killed, Sir Alexander Gordon and Charles

---

* The time of the Prussian arrival depends on how you define the Waterloo battlefield. They had been trudging their way on bad roads for more than twelve hours and had to take Plancenoit (about half a mile east of the road from Waterloo to Genappe) before attacking Napoleon's right flank. The Prussians arrived there at about 4.30 pm. The fighting was vicious, house-to-house and costly. Although the battle for Plancenoit involved more Prussians than Hougoumont involved Anglo-Allies, the effect was similar: the need for Napoleon to commit a significant number of men to the struggle, which reduced the forces facing Wellington to less than those at his disposal. (Adkin, pp. 379 ff.)

Fox Canning, were ADCs (Aides-De-Camp) to the Duke of Wellington – a prestigious but hazardous appointment, requiring them to be his eyes, ears and messengers. Of his other six ADCs, it is said that five were wounded and only one escaped unhurt.

Nivelles, June 19th 1815

My Dearest Mother

I take the earliest opportunity to tell you that we have had some very hard fighting, but that we have gained a most complete victory, and also that I am quite safe and have escaped unhurt. We removed from our quarters last Saturday week at Hérinnes and went to a village called Petit Rœulx, where we remained some time in quiet, but on Friday morning the 16th, at 2 o'clock, we were turned out & ordered to be under arms and ready to march at a moment's notice.

Accordingly we marched at 5 o'clock to Braine le Comte and then waited for a few hours for other troops to come up, then marched and took up a position close to this town [Nivelles] and about 4 leagues* from our original quarters. We had just begun to pitch our tents when we had another order to march on immediately against the French, who had attacked the Prussians in great force, three leagues farther on, near a village called Genappe.

Genappe is about 3 miles north of Quatre Bras, on the road from Brussels. Ligny, where the Prussians were engaged, is southeast of Quatre Bras and slightly to the south of the road from Nivelles

---

* Tom's use of 'leagues' as a measure of distance may seem rather quaint, but had a reason: one league, or 3 miles, was reckoned to be the average distance a man could walk in an hour. One way or another, Tom's estimate of 7 leagues for the actual route does not seem too far out.

to Namur. Three leagues is rather an underestimate of the distance from Nivelles to Ligny, but reasonably accurate for the distance from Nivelles to Quatre Bras, which Tom had to march.

We arrived there about five o'clock. The 1st Regiment [of Foot Guards] and Coldstreams* attacked the French with the bayonette and drove them back. We were kept as a reserve on the top of a hill, where we lay down in order to avoid the shots and shells, which were playing on us in great abundance. At 9 o'clock both parties ceased for want of light, but the French were driven back about half a league. The 1st Guards suffered much — had about 10 officers killed or wounded, and among the latter was Capt. Luttrell ,† but very slightly.

Skirmishing at Quatre Bras had started in the early morning, and the main French attack had got underway about three hours before the Guards arrived. On arrival both battalions of the 1st Foot Guards were immediately engaged and suffered heavy casualties, but managed to turn back the French advance.

Two very unfortunate accidents happened to them. They were charging a regiment of French, who came to a parley and said they would come over to us, but it was only a trick to wait for some cavalry which were coming on. They both attacked the 1st Guards together and repulsed them with a great loss. After

---

* Tom's reference to the Coldstreams relates only to their Light Companies, who had no casualties at all.

† Captain Francis Fownes-Luttrell, of the Light Company, 1st Foot Guards, was a cousin by marriage, which is no doubt why he is mentioned – see Biographical Notes in Appendix II for more details. His wound at Quatre Bras did not prevent him from fighting at Waterloo, where he was wounded again and seems to have lost an eye.

that they met with a French regiment who were cloaked in red, and did not find that they were French until too late, and in consequence were repulsed a second time. We only lost a few men from the shells, and we lay all night in the field without any cover in consequence of our baggage being left behind.

Next morning our regiment was sent into a wood to skirmish. We had a little fighting. About 5 o'clock we were obliged to retreat in consequence of the French having driven back the left wing, where the Prussians were placed. We went back and took up a position on the heights of St Jean, about 4 leagues back. The French returned in the evening, and cannonaded us till dark.

Tom then describes the battle of Waterloo itself, starting with the miserable conditions in which the army spent the night on Mont St Jean and the condition of the battlefield.

We all slept on the bare ground, with nothing either above or beneath us, in one of the most rainy nights possible, and before morning the ground on which we were was ankle-deep in mud. The French retired early in the morning, but came about 10 o'clock again in immense force. It is said they had 100,000 men, and we had at first 60,000 men, chiefly English,* excepting a few Dutch and Belgic, the chief part of whom ran away at the first attack.

The action commenced at about ½ past eleven by our artillery, which was drawn up about 20 yards before the first line, which was composed of our division and the 3rd Division† of the line.

---

* This statement is wholly inaccurate, but perhaps reflects the fact that Tom's division was entirely composed of British troops, apart from an artillery battery from the King's German Legion (KGL). In most cases the divisions were much more mixed, and deliberately so.

† The 3rd Division comprised one brigade of British infantry, one of the KGL and one Hanoverian. The Divisional artillery was partly British and partly KGL.

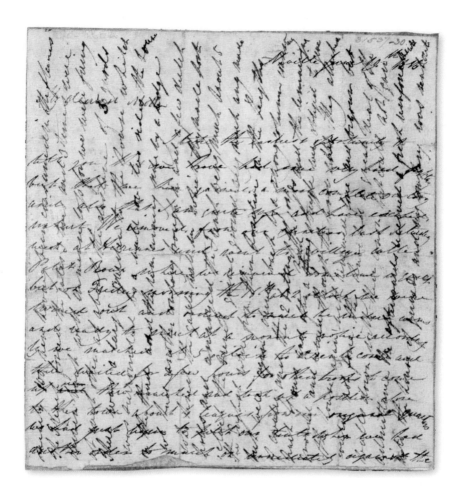

The first page of Tom's original letter, written the day after Waterloo. The practice of writing in two directions at 90 degrees across the sheet was common when paper was in short supply.

The French attacked a wood on our right, on the skirts of which there was a house, surrounded with a small wall, in which were placed the light infantry companies of the Coldstream Guards and our regiment, with orders to defend it to the last. The French were driven back, but advanced again with a fresh force, and succeeded in gaining entrance into the wood. They then sent fire-balls upon the house and set a barn and all the out-houses on fire.

After being exposed to a heavy fire of shot and grape and shells for two hours and a half, in which we had 3 officers wounded besides a number of men, the right wing of our regiment and my company went to the assistance of the Coldstreams in the wood, in which there was a very heavy fire of musquetry. The French were directing the whole of their fire at the house into which my company and another entered, nearly one hundred men having now been consumed in the flames.

The French forced the gates 3 times,* and 3 times were driven back with immense loss, for we were firing at one another at about 5 yards distance. There was a large garden to the house which was surrounded by a wall on 2 sides, the house on the 3rd, and on the remaining side a hedge. We had another company brought into it, and a few Dutch† who lined the garden wall, in which they made port-holes and annoyed the French very much.

About 5 o'clock the French gained ground very much and made the English retire from the position on the heights, but were again driven back by a strong column consisting of cavalry and

---

* 'This is a very interesting statement. There is certainly evidence of a second break in (see the evidence of Büsgen in *The Waterloo Archive, Vol 2* of this series), but this is the first statement to claim a third.' (Glover: *The Waterloo Archive, Vol 1*)

† These were German-speaking Nassauers. This is a pardonable mistake – as we have seen, they were actually part of the Netherlands army. However, they were certainly not few in number, even after casualties.

the 2nd and 3rd Battalions of the 1st Guards, and the remaining part of ours, and after a hard struggle were obliged to give ground and retreat through the wood. They attacked the house again with renewed force and vigour, but could not force it. The house had a great deal of the walls down with their cannon,* but they could not gain admittance. We afterwards received a fresh reinforcement of Guards into the house, and my company was sent out to skirmish. About 8 o'clock the first Guards and a part of ours charged the French with the bayonet and drove them entirely from the house. About that time a body of about 3000 Prussians came up,† and the French immediately retreated at a great pace, all our cavalry following them, with our regiments, drove them back double quick and dispersed them entirely.

My regiment has lost 16 officers killed and wounded, including Lieut-Col Sir A Gordon, and Canning of my company, who were among the number of killed. Capt Ashton of my company is also killed. The Duke of Wellington told us that he never saw soldiers behave so well as the Guards. The French have lost about 90 pieces of cannon and an immense number of killed and wounded.

The Belgic troops who ran away went to Brussels, where all our baggage was, and said that we were entirely defeated, and that the French were advancing close at their heels. The consequence was that the people of Brussels began to pillage our baggage, but were soon stopped. I understand that my baggage horse is either killed or stolen; but I do not know yet, as we have not seen the baggage since the 15th, and all that time we have been lying on the ground, without any covering and not able to change our clothes.

---

* 'This again proves that the French did pour cannon fire upon Hougoumont when able.' (Glover: op cit)

† Probably von Ziethen's I Corps – see above.

We have had nothing to eat, except a very little biscuit, and I have not tasted food now for 48 hours; but I am just going to have some, and I believe our baggage is to come up to-morrow. Another [trouble] is, that it is with the greatest difficulty we can get water, and what we did was horribly bad. I am now writing from the field in which we are to bivouac tonight, and therefore you must excuse the conciseness of this letter and I cannot get any more paper.

Good-bye, my dear mother, and believe me,

Yours most affectionately,

T Wedgwood

Tom's mother must have replied to this letter, but we do not know what she said. However, Bessy Wedgwood heard the news from their unmarried sister Emma, who was now living with John and Jenny, and wrote back on 28 June:

Oh how much I do sympathize with our dear sister Jenny upon what she must feel, not only hearing that her little hero is safe, but that he has behaved so well in this severe engagement and not the least of her pleasure … must be the consideration, the thought he shewed in writing from the field of battle to allay the fears of his family, and lastly his modesty, after all that he has gone through.[13]

In only nine days the news had travelled from Nivelles to John and Jenny's home in Exeter and then to Shrewsbury, where Bessy was visiting the Darwins.

Tom followed this up a few days later with two other letters. The first was once more to his mother and was probably sent as an insurance against the previous one going astray; by the time it was written, the

Anglo-Allied army had crossed into France. The dateline of Le Cateau is a reminder that the cockpit of Europe was not entirely confined to the boundaries of present day Belgium; almost one hundred years later, in August 1914, it would be the scene of a fighting withdrawal by the British Expeditionary Force during their retreat from Mons.

Tom Wedgwood to his mother Jenny Wedgwood – 24 June 1815

France
Encamped near Le Cateau
June 24th

My dear Mother

I sent a letter on the 19th to you from Nivelles by the post of the country which I do not think at all sure and therefore I write again to ease you from any anxiety you may have on my account as I am well, sound and in as high spirits as ever I was. You will have seen before this the account of the glorious victory we have had over the French. I believe the oldest soldier in the army never saw a more bloody or decisive battle. Bonaparte had the choice troops of his army and amazingly well they fought. At one time the victory was rather more than doubtful. The French had driven us from our position and excepting that part of the guards who were in a house in the wood the whole army was obliged to retreat to a short distance, but it was directly afterwards that the French were repulsed.

Bonaparte had 60,000 of the Guarde Imperiale all picked men. Part of them charged our Guards but were driven back with great slaughter. We had the post of honour and were the first to begin the attack. At the affair of the 16th [Quatre Bras] I was rather nervous at first, for we came quite unawares to the field after an amazing long march, and I had not time to get collected but soon got right again. On the 18th I did not feel at all in the same way, as we expected the action, and I was prepared. I trusted in God and He has been pleased to spare me, for which I hope I am as thankful as I ought.

The most disagreeable part was when we were on the top of our position, lying down doing nothing, with the shells and shot coming over like hailstones, and every now and then seeing 1 or 2 men killed. We had 2 officers wounded in that way. It was a very mournful sight next morning when I was on parade to see but little more than one-half the number of men that there were the morning before, and not quite one-half the officers.

The Duke of Wellington was very much pleased with us, but I do not believe he was so much so with the cavalry, as they did not do what was expected of them.

Our baggage was all sent to Brussels where a great deal of it was lost owing to a report which some of the Belgic troops spread that the French had entirely beat us and were close on their heels. I have lost a few things but some officers have lost everything they had. We were five days without any baggage tents or anything else, and you have no idea of what we underwent during that time, sleeping in the fields without even a hedge to cover us, generally raining the whole night and the ground ankle-deep in mud. I was 48 hours without eating anything, even a bit of biscuit, and having very often to send above a mile for water, but now we have got our baggage and tents and are much better off.

We are now about 8 leagues from the frontier, and are, I believe, to march straight for Paris. Most of the villages we pass through have the white flag hanging out, and Vive le Roi written on the houses. As yet we have found the people very civil, and they say they are very glad to see us. The Belgic troops behaved excessively bad, both in action and out, plundering and ill-treating the inhabitants. I wish they would send them back to their own country, I think they will do us more harm than good.

We have had two actions and they have run away both times. At the first action the Duke of Wellington was slightly wounded, and was saved being taken prisoner by the 92nd Regiment, who formed a square round him and by that means saved him.* My friend Vane with whom I lived so long in Brussels is wounded in the leg but not very bad. There is a young man of the name of Sim[p]son a friend of Mr Currey's was killed by a shot which took away nearly the whole of his back bone.† He was universally regretted for he was a very good natured as well as a gentlemanly young man. He came in the reg^t a short time after me.

It was a very curious circumstance that a little bit of meat which I was lucky enough to get the day before the last action I asked Capt^{ns} Ashton, Crawford, Forbes and Simpson to partake with me, which they did, and the next day I was the only one of the 5 who was left alive.

If we have any action you must not be uneasy for me if I do not write immediately as it is not always possible but whenever it is

---

* Wellington was famous for his 'hands-on' approach to generalship and was not afraid of putting himself into danger. This probably refers to an incident at Quatre Bras when he narrowly escaped by getting his horse to leap over the 92nd while they were crouching in a roadside ditch. It was a less formal manoeuvre than Tom describes, and there are no other reports of Wellington having been wounded.

† The unfortunate Ensign Simpson was struck while lying down for shelter on the ridge and lingered on until the evening – Tom spared his mother from the most harrowing of the details. See also Biographical Notes in Appendix II.

you may depend on it, you shall hear from me. I have been looking out for a letter for sometime past but have not received any but you must let me hear from you very soon and with my best love to all friends.

Your most affectionate son
T Wedgwood

I have written a couple of times to Allen to let him know I am well.

Tom added a further postscript three days later, when they had reached the Somme and were roughly halfway to Paris.

<u>June 27th</u> I have kept this letter waiting for an opportunity to send it. We have this morning crossed the river Somme and are in a village called Bedoincourt near Ham.* Our division took the town of Péronne last night with very little loss.

The strategically important town of Péronne lay on the Somme and was taken by the 1st Foot Guards, together with the Light Companies of all four Guards battalions, which were brigaded together in the same way as they had been at Hougoumont.

The town had previously rejoiced in the informal name of Péronne la Pucelle, meaning that it had never been taken; Wellington is said to have smiled when reminded that he had broken that record.[14] It surrendered after putting up no more than a token resistance, which was probably very sensible. Wellington had issued a General Order

---

* Ham is a small town on the Somme; it has been impossible to identify Bedoincourt with certainty. Most probably it is a misreading for Berlancourt, south of Ham. Another possibility is Bethencourt, about 5 miles down river and quite close to Péronne. This seems less likely, as Tom writes of crossing the river rather than staying near it, and Bethencourt is actually further north than Ham. According to Siborne, however, Berlancourt was on the Prussian line of advance, rather than the British. But both lines were quite close at that point.

to treat the ordinary French population as if they were members of a Coalition nation – in other words, the enemy was Napoleon rather than France – but this generosity might have worn thin if more resistance had been shown; the British casualties have been estimated at one dead and twelve wounded, of which two were officers.[15]

Péronne was to be devastated fifty-five years later, during the Franco-Prussian War, and again in 1917.

Tom Wedgwood to his uncle, Lancelot Baugh Allen – 4 July 1815

The next letter is particularly interesting because it provides the clearest description of Tom's movements in the days leading up to the Battle of Waterloo. It was written while the British forces were encamped just outside Paris, waiting for the final surrender terms to be agreed, and addressed to his uncle Lancelot Baugh Allen. Known in the family as Baugh, he was almost certainly instrumental in getting Tom into the army. He had qualified in the law and, reading between the lines, it is also likely that he was consulted on financial and other matters.

The letter also appears in *A Century of Family Letters*, but with abridgements which have been restored in the version set out below. In this case, they were probably made on the grounds of not being very interesting, but the passage of another century rather alters the perspective.

Le Bourget
July 4th 1815

My dear Uncle

I have just received your kind letter and which I dare say you did not think at the time you wrote it that it would reach me close to Paris which we are to enter on the 6th in spite of your prediction to the contrary. I will now give you a short sketch of our movements since we left Hérinnes at least of that part of the Army to which I belong as I daresay you know the accounts better than myself of the motions of the army in general.

As well as I recollect we left Hérinnes on the 11th of June in order to make room for some cavalry and marched to the villages of Steenkirk and Petit Rœulx 3 leagues rather to the left of Enghien and about the same distance from the Frontier. We heard reports on the evening of the 15th that the French had attacked the Prussian outposts and driven them near Nivelles.

At 1 o'clock in the morning of the 16 which I think was the most fatiguing day I ever experienced we had orders to remain under arms, and consequently the battalion assembled at Petit Rœulx and remained there till 4 when we received orders to march to Braine le Comte and there wait for the remainder of the division about a league we waited there 2 or 3 hours and then marched to a position on the heights of Nivelles rather better than 3 leagues.

We had just begun to pitch our tents when we received a fresh order to advance again. We at that time heard a very heavy cannonade. We marched on 2 leagues further and came to a field of action near the Village of Genappe between 4 and 5. The 1st and Colds advanced to the attack immediately and we were kept as a Corps of reserve under cover of a hill. The 1st regiment suffered very much. Our reg was only under fire of some shells and balls, and only lost 7 or 8 men. At 9 the action ceased. We having driven the French a little way back. We laid down on the ground till 2 o'clock when my regt marched into a wood close by us on the right and lined the bank with men by the side of the enemies' positions from which we were but a few hundred yards. The French Pickets observed us moving and fired at us but only hit 3 or 4 men. Our men had orders to lie down on the inside of

Lancelot Baugh Allen

the hedge and not to fire till they came within a few yards.

About 6 the French Columns moved to our left without troubling us except by a little skirmishing. About 11 we had orders to retreat out of the wood to take up a position on the heights of St Jean close to the village of Waterloo 3 leagues back and about 2 to the left of Nivelles. The French followed us in the evening and shelled us a little which was returned by our artillery, we remained quiet that night and early on the 18 we saw the whole of the French army in motion and soon lost sight of them, however they soon reappeared and formed for battle.

Our division was formed in squares on the brow of the heights with the guns belonging to it in our front about 10 yards. There was a wood on our right at the bottom of the hill on the skirts of which was a large farm its house surrounded with a thin wall which also extended round that part of a large garden which faced the enemy. In this house was placed the light companies of the Colds and ours under the command of Lt Col McDonall with orders to defend it to the last.

At ½ past 11 the French advanced with 2 battalions to attack the wood into which the Colds had previously occupied. The battle begun by our artillery playing upon those French who were soon driven back from the wood but advanced again considerably reinforced especially with a number of Guns. They then got into the wood. The remainder of our division was laid down upon the ground to avoid the shot and shell which came with abundance. We had 2 officers wounded and 1 killed in that way. The latter was Ensign Simpson I believe a friend of Mr Curries. He had the whole of his backbone taken away by a shot which also killed a sergeant and more near him.

My regt kept moving down to the wood by 2 companies at a time. I went down about 2 o'clock and found the shots flying annoyingly thick. After being some time in an orchard firing at the French my company went into the farmhouse where there were most part of the 2 regts. The French fired fire balls at the house and put all the out houses on fire, after that they attacked the gates [and] broke in but were driven back, which was repeated, 3 times with the same success. There was an immense carnage at that time for we were firing at each other across a yard and charging them with the bayonette. We all remained in this house till the end of the action (except making frequent sallies) which ended at dusk.

Next day we marched to Nivelles and nothing has happened since then to our arrival here which was last Saturday [1 July] except the taking of a few small towns. Our division took Péronne by storm with hardly any loss. I saw several beautiful charges of cavalry especially one where almost a whole regt of Cuirassiers were cut to pieces.

We went under amazing hardships for the first few days. We had no baggage. On the 17th during the time we marched the heat was intense, just as we halted a thunder storm came on which lasted for 3 hours and wet us who were without any covering to the skin and also made the ground very wet for we were on a potato field and it was nearly ankle deep in mud. To add to our misery we could get nothing to eat or drink not even water except what fell from the clouds and with the greatest difficulty made 1 or 2 small fires we laid down on this ground when it set dark and it rained the whole night very hard. I did not taste a bit of anything for 48 hours, not even a bit of biscuit.

We bivouacked in that way for 5 nights without tent or baggage [which] was sent to Brussels at the commencement of the action, some of the Belgic troops ran away and spread a report in Brussels that we were defeated and the French close at their heels. The consequence was that the baggage of the Army as well as Stores made a rush to get out of town with the greatest disorder. An immense quantity of baggage was lost. The Belgians whenever they saw any fall from a horse immediately plundered it. I lost a port manteau in which were all my books and John Allen* his besides other things.

On the evening of the 15th I felt rather nervous just as you describe Tom Allen† to have been. We went into action without the least idea of it except about 1 hour meeting on our march

---

* Probably his uncle, who inherited Cresselly in 1803, rather than Tom's brother John Allen Wedgwood – see Biographical Notes in Appendix I.

† It has proved impossible to trace Tom Allen with certainty – see Biographical Notes in Appendix I.

all the wounded men, and we lay down for 2 or 3 hours doing nothing. I had not time to prepare for it, but afterwards I felt perfectly at my ease.

Belgic troops did not behave well at either action. At first they ran off entirely and afterwards took every opportunity of getting away. We met on the road very often 6 men with one that was wounded slightly all going to Nivelles 2 leagues off and always a great many more than was necessary. If one of them had his musquet broke or expended his ammunition he went away. And for all that time they call themselves the Braves Belges and take most part of the credit to themselves. The Brussels news papers are full of accounts of the prodigies of valour performed by these Braves Belges.

Tom added a postscript three days later, when they had encamped in the Bois de Boulogne. What Tom does not refer to, and clearly did not realise, was that Louis XVIII had been restored to the throne on that very day, thus probably accounting for the royalists who wished to enter the city.

Le Bois de Boulogne
July 8th

On the 5th we moved from Le Bourget and occupied the heights of Mont Martre. The next day we sent strong piquets to each of the gates of Paris to take possession of them but did not enter the town as we expected. I was on piquet at 1 of them. We had orders to prevent any party, officer or soldier or indeed any thing belonging to the Allied army from entering the town, but not to meddle with the French as there was also a party of the National Guard there.

A party of French Royalists came in the night and insisted upon entering which the National Guard refused and the

Royalists proceeded to break the gates open, but upon our explaining to the officer commanding the royalists that none of the allies were in Paris and that there was a particular order that they were not to enter. He said that as an Englishman told him so it was sufficient and he withdrew his troops outside.

We encamped here and I believe are likely to stay here some time. The gates of Paris were opened to us and we all dined there. Our camp is but ½ a mile from the Barrière.

I was not aware you had been so unwell, but am glad to hear that you are so much better and I hope this warm weather will do you good. I have not heard from Allen since we first marched nor have I wrote to him since the 19th there being no communication between France and Holland. I hope you will be able to make out this writing. Pray remember me kindly to Mr Currie * and believe me

Yours most sincerely
T Wedgwood

In those days the 'Portes de Paris' had more than symbolic meaning and were represented by Barrières, which were formal customs posts. Some of these, often of rather grand architecture, remain standing today.

* Probably related to Sir Edmund Currey, responsible for getting Tom his commission – see Biographical Notes in Appendix I.

Tom Wedgwood to William Siborne – 12 March 1835

There is one other letter relating to the battle which is worth reproducing here, although it was written twenty years after the event. In 1830, William Siborne, a junior officer who had not actually been present at Waterloo, obtained a grant from the Government to construct a model of the battlefield. One of the reasons, perhaps, was that by then the ground had been radically altered by the construction of the Lion Mound. As part of this process, he sent a circular letter to all known surviving officers, asking if they could supply information. He was especially interested in what they were doing at about 7.00 pm, when the final attack of the French Imperial Guard was at its height, as this was the event that the model would portray.

Tom replied from Maer Hall, which was the home of Jos and Bessy. He was still unmarried at the time, and was probably spending his leave with them.

Maer Hall
March 12th 1835

Sir

I answer to your circular, which in consequence of my being absent from my regiment, I have only just received, I am sorry to state that I am unable to give you any information, that could be in the least useful to you. On the evening of the 18th of June, I was myself stationed almost entirely within the walls of the Château & garden or else in the orchard and wood immediately outside and am quite ignorant of the nature of the crops growing in its vicinity, with the exception that they were chiefly standing corn.

To the best of my recollection, the 2nd Battalion 3rd Guards was, about 7 p.m. stationed within the walls of the Château, but were at that time not much pressed by the enemy. I remember, that I was myself completely ignorant of what was going on, or what the result of the action was likely to be until we saw parties of the French passing us in full retreat, with the Brunswickers in pursuit on both sides of the house.

I believe there was a large gateway, to which the road through the wood, led, which is not marked on the plan sent.

I have the honor to be

Sir

Your obedt & humble servant

T Wedgwood, Capt & Lt Col

3rd FGds

PARIS, 1815

A week later, Tom wrote to his father to tell him what had been happening. On the actual day of Tom's letter, Napoleon, who had been at large since the Battle of Waterloo, finally surrendered to the captain of HMS *Bellerophon*. That news had clearly not come through. But 'all the Emperors and Kings' had arrived in Paris to start negotiating the agreement that eventually became the Second Treaty of Paris.

At a more mundane level, Tom describes an intriguing meeting with a 'Welchwoman', the sister of Jenny's first cousin James Allen. In Tom's next letter it turns out that her married name is Collos: her husband was a French officer who had been in the abortive – not to mention bizarre – landing at Fishguard in 1797. He was taken prisoner but was granted parole and earned his living as a music master in Tenby; Jenny's father forbade his daughters to see them, which is presumably why Tom had no idea who they were. M Collos (we are never told their Christian names) returned to Paris with his wife, most likely during the Peace of Amiens in 1802–3, and opened a fish shop in the rue de la Grande Truanderie. In 1818 Josiah II, Bessy and their four daughters visited them in Paris, but it is evident that relations with Mme Collos were still rather strained.[16]

Tom Wedgwood to his father John Wedgwood – 15 July 1815

Paris
July 15th 1815

My dear Father

Many thanks for your welcome letters which I received on Thursday as it will enable me to see all the curiosities of this great town. I must also thank you for your other letters which I can assure you were very acceptable.

We have now been in the neighbourhood of Paris for some time. On the 5th we advanced from our position and occupied that of the French according to the convention. Our division was at La Villette which is close to the Barrière of Paris. On the 7th we removed to the Bois de Boulogne and encamped in it, about ½ a league from the Barrière de Neuilly. We have remained there ever since but we are so near Paris that we are always there. I have taken a room with another officer where we go immediately after parade and return to the camp at night.

All the Emperors and Kings are now in Paris. I was on guard at the Emperor of Russia's on the 13th. He treated us very generously. The guard consisted of 100 men; he gave them 150 lbs of meat, 200 lbs of bread, 100 bottles of very good wine, and vegetables. The officers had an excellent dinner and might call at any time for anything. We had a very pleasant dinner. We had an Englishman who had been 25 years in the Russian service. He was chief physician to the Emperor and to the whole of His army.*

About the middle of dinner Platoff† came in and sat with us for a couple of hours and talked with us quite familiarly. He said he enjoyed his visit to England more than anything in his life, and that he liked the English women better than any others, and when he went out he shook us by the hand most heartily. I do not know the name of the Englishman but he was knighted by the Prince Regent [in] London and afterwards made Baronet on board the Impregnable. He told us that the Russians had vowed not to leave a house in Paris standing if they met with any opposition and

---

* Probably Sir James Wylie (1768–1854).

† 'Hetman of the Cossacks' (Glover)

as to the Cossacks they had determined to give no quarter. He also said that the English were very much liked by the Russians. Indeed I find we are liked by all troops except the Belgians and the French like us much better than any others.

I have not had time to see Paris sufficiently to compare it with London. There are certainly much finer buildings and walks in the former but then the latter beats them out and out in streets and rides and also I think in comforts.

As yet I have only seen the Louvre which is only open to the military, the French Theatre, and the Garden of the Thuilleries. I think the Louvre is the most beautiful thing I ever saw both in and outside. There is no use my describing it to you for you must know it much better than I do. I was in the rue Neuve des Petits Champs in a very good situation and street. It leads at one end to the Place Vendôme and there is an entrance at the other into the Palais Royal and it is also close to the Thuilleries.

I think the French are the most impertinent and most civil people in the world. As a proof of the latter, I was on guard at one of the gates of Paris and had black crape round my arm. A gentleman with two women came up to me in a very civil way and beseeched to know what was the meaning of the crape round my arm. I told them, but that was not sufficient for they asked who for, which made me stare, however I told them and walked away.

I rather think I met the same day the sister of Mr James Allen whom you mention in your letter. I was accosted by a woman in English and among other things she told me she was a Welchwoman but not knowing that Mr James Allen had a sister in Paris it of course did not strike me.

This 3 weeks' campaigning has only affected me in one way, it made my legs very sore. For the first 3 days I did [not] take off my boots and they got wet several times and dried again on my feet, and when I got them off at last, I could not get them on again without cutting the leather half way down my foot, the consequence was that the insteps of my feet were made quite raw. There is also another thing which I cannot account for in the least. My face is quite contracted on one side; and when I smile my mouth gets quite to the left side of my face, and when I eat my upper jaw does not come exactly on my under one, and I cannot shut one of my eyes without the other, which I could do before; however I do not feel it quite so much as before.

What is Charles's direction at his academy for I want to write to him.

I lost a small portmanteau with my books and some clothes in it but I was very glad to recover the rest as I had heard that my horse and baggage was all lost.

There are detachments of 200 men for each batt^n of guards on the march to join us and we expect them in about 10 days. They are a day after the fair.

Pray remember me to M^r and Mrs Templer * and believe me my dear Father

Your most affectionate son
T Wedgwood

Henrietta Litchfield added that 'his face never entirely recovered from the paralysis brought on by exposure and want of food'.

This seems medically unlikely and Philip Kerry's research suggests that the cause was Bell's Palsy, possibly due to a viral inflammation of a cranial nerve.[17] It is named after the eminent surgeon Sir Charles Bell, who amongst other things was a founder of the Middlesex

---

* George Templer was the active partner in Davison's bank, in which John had invested – see page 24.

Hospital Medical School and a friend of Francis Horner, who appears in Tom's next letter.

Bell had also made his name in military circles by attending the wounded who had returned to England from Corunna in 1809 – one result of this was a paper on gunshot wounds, which he published as part of a work on operative surgery. He added to this in 1815 by dashing out to Belgium when Brussels was overwhelmed with casualties from both sides, and was put in charge of a hospital. Although the number of his actual operations has been disputed,[18] he is said to have attended about 300 over three successive days and nights[19] – and on top of this found time to draw some extremely graphic illustrations of battlefield injuries.

The overall success rate of his operations is reported to have been typical of the times, with about a three in four chance of survival where complications had not set in, dropping to just under one in two where gangrene or other infections were present;[20] interestingly the statistics for survival once the wounded had actually arrived at hospital (an important point) were not much worse than those of World War I.[21]

Tom Wedgwood to his uncle, Baugh Allen – 14 August 1815

The final letter of 1815 is another one to his uncle. The opening paragraph seems hardly surprising, given the privations of the previous month.

Bois de Boulogne
August 14th

My dear Uncle

I have seen Dr Curriey who gave me your letter which proved very welcome and I shall trouble him to carry this one back to you. I am now quite well but have been ill for some time with a fever and bad headaches, they kept me in camp for a week and then I was confined another week by boils which broke out all over my face and body. Yesterday was the first day I could put on my clothes properly. The contraction in my face has entirely left me.

Sir John Byng* has not yet taken any notice of me. He is esteemed to be a very good officer and is much liked by our brigade. I am very much obliged to you for writing to him about me.

I delivered yesterday a letter to Mons[r] *le Chevalier which my father sent me some time ago and which he got from M*[r] *Horner.† He was very kind, and lent me some French books to read. He also promised that as soon as we were in Paris (which we expected to be very soon) he would introduce me to a Young French Gentleman who would shew me every thing in Paris and also read with me, by which means we should be mutually improved in French & English which he is learning. He speaks very highly of the English and says that he was happier at Dulwich than he has been since.*

---

* General Sir John Byng was in command of the 2nd Guards Brigade, which included Tom's battalion. Baugh had obviously put in a good word for him.

† A Whig statesman and family friend. As noted earlier, he was also a friend of Sir Charles Bell, who wrote him a very descriptive letter about the condition of the wounded at Waterloo. See Biographical Notes in Appendix I, under *Friends of the Family.*

I have been so much confined with one thing or another that I have not been able to see much in Paris. However I have seen most of the celebrated sights. The Louvre is beautiful, of which I shall never be tired. In it there is the original from which the painting over the altar in Dulwich Chapel is copied and they call it the masterpiece of Raphael. There are also the 3 masterpieces of sculpture but I like the Apollo better than the other two there is some thing in it that strikes one directly.

I have been to the theatre several times and like the Acting pretty well. I find I can understand them much better than I could. The theatres themselves are very inferior to the English both in size and beauty. I have seen Madame Collos 3 times and dine there Sunday where I am to meet the two Ridgways* whom I never saw. She expressed a great desire to see them and I wrote a letter and sent it to their reg^t.† Since then they have called there. The youngest was wounded at Waterloo and has lost a finger. I was there yesterday and gave her your message. She says that the best way to come here is by going down to Brighton and crossing over to Dieppe. Me Collos says that by that means you will save a day and a half and perhaps 2 days and also that the travelling is much better from Dieppe than Calais.

She said that James Allen said he would come over this month and she had recommended the same way to him. I enquired from Mr Collos about the roads down to Aix. He says he believes they are perfectly safe now. It is expected very soon that the armies will go into quarters over the different provinces, when that takes place I should think there would be no doubt of the safety of travelling every where.

---

* Probably Allen relations – see Biographical Notes in Appendix I.

† See Biographical Notes in Appendix I.

My father mentioned in his last letter that Jos* would be in Paris soon. I hope he will. I have written a letter to Mr Currey and shall give it with t[w]o to D^r C to take to England.

I find my mother is going down to Staffordshire with Elizabeth.† I am very glad of it for besides the pleasure it gives her, she is generally much better after those jaunts.

The Bois de Boulogne is nearly quite spoilt now in its appearance by the troops who are encamped in it. They have cut down most of the trees to make […]. All the officers of our division are quartered in 2 […] which are on each side of the gate leading into […]. It is better than being in tents altho' we are very much crowded. We are near ½ a mile to the Barrière de Neuilly which leads into the Champs Elysées at the bottom of which are the Thuilleries.

We find the Emperor of Russia's guard in general. He lives in one of Bonaparte's palaces and has all his wines. He treats that whole guard magnificently giving the men each a bottle of wine and as much meat, bread and vegetables as they can eat and very often money. The officers dine with the Emperor's Staff and can call for anything they like during the day. I have nothing more to add but my wishes for your health and believe me to be

Yours most affectionately
T Wedgwood

---

* Probably Tom's cousin, Josiah III, rather than his uncle, Josiah II.

† Probably his older sister Sarah Elizabeth Wedgwood, generally known as Eliza. In the words of Henrietta Litchfield, 'she was an invalid, but though she was thought to be a "fading flower", lived to the age of 62'. The reference to being 'generally much better' is probably to her, although it might possibly relate to his mother who could have been worried about John's financial position – a problem about to reach crisis point in 1816.

Baugh Allen was initially Warden and then, from 1811, Master of Dulwich College, which is obviously why Tom mentions it. At the time the surname Allen was a pre-requisite for the job, although there is no suggestion that he was actually related to the founder.

Another requirement was being unmarried. Two years earlier Baugh had devised a plan to change the regulations by Act of Parliament, but the Bill was not carried and Baugh did not marry until six years later, in 1820, at which point he resigned the Mastership.[22]

As a result, Dulwich College lost a talented man. He had improved the college estates and income, and was responsible for establishing the Dulwich Picture Gallery in its present form. The history is slightly complicated, but essentially a collection accumulated for the King of Poland was looking for a permanent home, as Poland no longer existed as an independent state. The Royal Academy had turned it down when the owner met Baugh at a dinner party. The College already had a dilapidated picture gallery which was about to be restored and some money had been set aside for the purpose, but it was agreed that the collection should come to the College, housed in a new building towards which the owner also contributed.[23]

A peace treaty with France was finally signed on 20 November. Under its terms there was to be an army of occupation, to which Britain would contribute 30,000 men; but this time there was no difficulty in meeting that commitment as fresh troops had at last arrived from Canada, having – and no doubt to their great annoyance – been too late to join in the battle. In mid-December, Tom and his battalion marched to Boulogne and sailed for home.

TOM'S WATERLOO MEDALS

At the beginning of the nineteenth century, the idea of awarding official medals for service or gallantry had not taken hold, although long service, battles and campaigns, individual acts of gallantry or other meritorious service were sometimes marked by the issue of medals paid for by commanding officers or fellow soldiers. This did not change in principle until the Victoria Cross was instituted in 1856. However, after the Battle of Waterloo public pressure led the government to grant a medal, on application, to those who been present at any of the actions between 16 and 18 June 1815: about 37,000 such medals were eventually awarded.

Tom received one of these campaign medals, which is now back in family ownership.

The second, more intriguing, medal was the subject of a most impressive study by Philip Kerry, in *He Fought at Waterloo: Thomas Josiah Wedgwood*[24] and to which this work is much indebted. The reverse is engraved as follows:

Subscribed to
by Officers of the
2nd Batt 3rd Regt Foot Gds
And presented to
ENSIGN WEDGWOOD
for his Gallant Action at
WATERLOO
June 18th 1815

Unfortunately, there is no further information on the nature of his 'Gallant Action' and his letters provide no clue. Indeed, there remains

*Tom's Waterloo medals. On the left is the general Waterloo medal
(with miniature) and on the right is the one said to have been
presented by his fellow officers.*

a lingering suspicion that the medal is actually bogus and Philip Kerry has since indicated that around the end of the nineteenth century faking Waterloo medals had become quite an industry.

If genuine, Kerry suggests that Tom was possibly awarded the medal for carrying the Battalion Colours. That duty was regarded as a high honour, even if it was somewhat hazardous: the Colours would be a natural target, and holding them up would impede the bearer's chance of defending himself. For that reason, they were normally escorted by a Colour Party of four sergeants armed with pikes.

The question of who actually carried the colours at Waterloo is unclear. Kerry says that the Colours were normally carried by Ensigns of the 5th Company. It would make practical sense, as the Colours were carried at the centre of the battalion when formed in line and would therefore be between the Nos 4 and 5 Companies. Tom was in the 5th Company, and if he can be confirmed as one of those who carried the colours at some stage during the battle, it could explain the medal.

We know, however, that the 7th and 8th Companies of the 2/Coldstream remained on the ridge as Colour Guard while the other companies were fed into Hougoumont,[25] and Adkin suggests that the 2/3rd Guards probably adopted the same policy. It seems very unlikely that the Colours would have been taken into Hougoumont, but this does not preclude Tom from having performed that duty at an earlier stage in the battle. However, one might expect him to have mentioned something about this role – even if he generally says very little about his personal involvement in the fighting.

AFTER WATERLOO

POLITICAL AND SOCIAL TENSION

Napoleon, the 'Great Disturber of Europe', had been confined. Tom remained in the army but had returned to a country beset with economic, social and political problems. Government policy did not then extend to considering the necessary transition from a war economy; Income Tax, which had been introduced to pay for the war, was repealed and military expenditure was immediately scaled down. Combined with massive interest payments on the national debt, this produced an economic crisis, possibly short term but still enough of a shock to send banks, including the one in which Tom's father was a partner, into insolvency.

Natural disasters did not help. 1816 was the 'Year Without a Summer', now thought to have been caused by a volcanic eruption in Indonesia, and it was followed by two or three further years of bad harvests. The resulting strain on the poor was increased by the Corn Laws, designed to keep grain prices high.

The political structures of Britain had effectively frozen; at the highest level the situation resulted in calls for political reform and at the lowest and most immediate in civil unrest. Less than eighteen months after Waterloo, there were protest meetings at Spa Fields in London. On the first occasion, the event passed off relatively peacefully but the second was slightly more serious. The rudimentary system of civilian policing was not enough to deal with the problem and, inevitably, the military were called in to keep order. The Guards do not seem to have been actively concerned, even though they tended to be based in the capital, but as a precaution their normal six-monthly rotation from one barracks to another was postponed for a few days.[26]

Disturbances continued during the following years, often in manufacturing towns. The 'Peterloo Massacre' of August 1819 in Manchester, when the Yeomanry charged into the crowd, killing fifteen people and wounding hundreds of others, was in very broad terms partly about the Corn Laws, partly about wage cuts and partly about suffrage. It was followed the next year in London by the Cato Street Conspiracy, a much more focussed plan to murder the Prime Minister and the entire Cabinet. This was forestalled by the Government, and a company of the Coldstreams took part in the arrests, but there seems to have been no other direct involvement of the Guards.

Unrest even extended, in a rather more mild way, to the Guards themselves. Acting on behalf of the civil power was unpopular, because the soldiers had to put up with a great deal of provocation and, unlike the yeomanry, their training and discipline made this hard to bear; indeed, there were apparently cases where they had to endure legal action when protesters were killed or injured.[27] Shortly after Cato Street, the left wing of the 1/3rd Guards (Tom's regiment, but not his battalion) exhibited discontent by refusing to obey orders; it seems that this was partly in protest at their transfer from relatively easy-going billets to overcrowded and inconvenient barracks,* and partly at deductions from pay and the failure to pay them various allowances – not to mention drinking-money for the King's birthday. They were briskly marched off to Portsmouth and everything was smoothed over, but it was a very worrying moment for the authorities.[28]

Pre-occupation with domestic issues probably meant that most of the British public let foreign problems pass them by, but some of these were much more serious. Revolutionary enthusiasm and the power

---

* These barracks were the King's Mews, quite literally converted stables, which had been rushed into service and stood on the site of the present day National Gallery. A possible contributory factor was that the officers were quartered elsewhere and therefore out of touch with what was going on.

vacuum created when Napoleon was finally deposed had left many countries in an unstable condition. The duc de Berry, whom we met just before Waterloo, was assassinated in Paris and there was also unrest in the 'Two Sicilies', at Naples and Palermo.

Trouble extended further west as well. Spain had adopted a liberal constitution in 1812, only to have it rejected two years later when Ferdinand VII returned to the throne. Eventually, the Spanish army mutinied in favour of a more liberal regime, but this was suppressed with French support and an absolute monarchy continued in power. Neighbouring Portugal went through similar problems, although the outcome was somewhat more liberal.

A few years later a combination of these Iberian events was to affect Tom personally.

Pressure for reform continued in Britain, especially in the industrial north, but the Guards do not seem to have been seriously involved in further civil policing and reverted to a more steady routine. Many regiments spent long years overseas garrisoning the expanding British Empire, but the Guards remained largely in England because of their public duties. As well as their main barracks in the capital, postings included royal residences, and smaller detachments were also sent to the militarily important dockyards; by 1827, Tom had served in four of them.[29]

Ireland, however, was a growing problem, and so Dublin came into the cycle from 1821.[30] It was not a posting that Tom looked forward to, although his reasons are not clear: perhaps it was the political atmosphere, but it might equally have been the relatively limited social opportunities.[31] As an aside, it is interesting to see that troops destined for Ireland sometimes travelled to Liverpool or Manchester by canal and then took ship; the Grand Union Canal had made Paddington an important hub some years before the railways arrived – and it would be nice to think that part of their route followed the Trent and Mersey Canal, promoted by Tom's grandfather, Josiah I. Similarly, when posted to a dockyard, the Guards might sail from a port nearer London.[32]

Otherwise, there was a great deal of marching.

PORTUGAL

IBERIAN POLITICS

This pattern lasted for slightly more than ten years, during which Tom had become a Lieutenant & Captain.* In late 1826, however, he was posted to Portugal as part of a small peace-keeping force, and over the next fifteen months he kept his family up to date by means of a journal. It has none of the drama of his Waterloo letters, but it does provide a detailed view of his experiences and opinions and is easily the best insight into his character that we have.

The background, put briefly, was this: Portugal had been an absolute monarchy until Napoleon invaded it in 1807 and instituted his own form of absolutism, upon which the Portuguese Court fled to Brazil and remained there for some years after he was defeated. In the meantime, liberal sentiments were growing in Portugal itself and a certain amount of political reform took place after a revolt in 1820; the Court then returned to Portugal and a moderately liberal constitution was adopted in 1822.

However, the situation was fragile and what became known as the 'Liberal Wars' were about to start in earnest. On the face of it this was a dispute about succession following the death of the Portuguese king, John IV. The roots were more complicated, however, and included the growing economic strength and newly declared independence of Brazil, a dysfunctional royal family and more than a whiff of revolutionary zeal.

---

* This was by purchase, as was then the system, and cost £1,200 – a fair amount in those days, although he would have covered some of it from the sale of his ensigncy. Most probably, he was helped by one of his uncles.

In theory, the new monarch was Donna Maria, a seven-year-old princess whose aunt acted as Regent; but the real power resided with the old Queen Mother, a true Bourbon, who had learned nothing and forgotten nothing, and was absolutist to the core. Her relations in Spain sided actively with the absolutist rebels, who wished to put her second son, Dom Miguel – already in exile for attempting a coup against his father a couple of years earlier – on the throne.*

For some years the country had effectively been a British protectorate. Canning, then Foreign Secretary and once ambassador to Portugal, concluded that the involvement of Spain constituted interference in Portugal's internal affairs and therefore justified a British response. In one of the greatest speeches of his career, he persuaded Parliament and the King 'to fly to the aid of Portugal … not to rule, not to dictate, not to prescribe constitutions, but to defend and preserve the independence of an ally. We go to plant the standard of England on the well known heights of Lisbon – where that standard is planted, foreign dominion shall not come'[33] and in less than three weeks about 5,000 British troops, with naval support, were despatched to Portugal.†

COMMITMENT OF BRITISH TROOPS

While the numbers may not seem large today, this was quite a logistical feat. There had been at least two major rounds of army cuts

---

* His elder brother, Pedro IV, had abdicated his right to the Portuguese throne, but remained Emperor of Brazil. Part of the agreement was that Miguel would marry King John IV's daughter – and Miguel's niece – who would succeed Pedro as queen in her own right. A suitable dispensation was no doubt obtained from the Pope. Such marriages were not uncommon in the Portuguese royal family. John IV himself was the result of a marriage between an uncle and a niece: of the resulting seven children, four were either stillborn or survived for no more than a year or two.

† Further details of the regiments and senior officers involved are given in Appendix V.

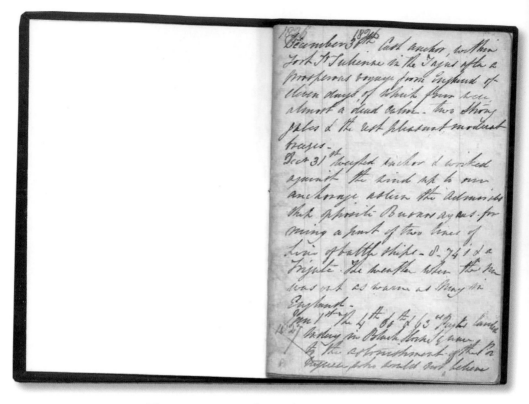

The opening page of Tom's Portuguese journal

since 1815; the Coldstreams, for example, had been reduced to about half of their Waterloo strength.[34] Resources were already stretched and as a result the expedition required the movement of significantly more troops than were actually sent overseas.

The Guards provided about a quarter of the force, perhaps because their ceremonial duties were easier to re-arrange. Such involvement had clearly been anticipated, for no more than a day or two after Canning's speech the 3rd Guards were marching down Birdcage Walk to the sound of their band and cheers from the public;[35] but after that exhilarating send-off the route became a long hard slog to Portsmouth, 25 miles a day over heavy roads, in the middle of December.

Typically, the soldiers' wives and children followed a regiment to its port of departure, even if they had not been taken 'on the strength' – that is, employed as cooks and washerwomen. One report puts the number arriving in Portsmouth as in their hundreds, and describes the heart-rending scenes of distress at their husbands' departure, adding – without further comment – that two children of the 63rd Regiment had died of fatigue while on the road.[36]

Officers' wives were a different matter, but on the whole the officers, like Tom, were still unmarried. Those who were tended to be quite senior and, most likely, the army did not really know how to deal with matters if their wives intended to come along as well. It was said that Lady Bouverie, whose husband commanded the Guards Brigade, delayed the departure of their ship by a day;[37] and Tom records that a few months later a parade in the blazing sun was eventually cancelled because her riding habit was not ready. Whether or not these stories were true, Tom had a low opinion of her, but wisely kept it to himself and his journal.[38]

Against this, the other wife mentioned by Tom, very recently married to his friend Henry Montagu,* had a most agreeable and adaptable nature – and was also rather pretty. The couple had married while preparations for departure were at their height; exactly when he sailed is not entirely clear, but was at the most two days afterwards. Tom says that they were 'immediately parted' after the wedding ceremony, which was held in London, but even so Montagu would have had very little time to get down to Portsmouth. Mrs Montagu followed her husband to Portugal about six months later, leaving him racked with apprehension when her ship – a steamboat carrying a 'cargo of

---

* Montagu and Tom were almost exactly the same age, and both had fought at Waterloo. Up to this point, he does not seem to have been a particular friend, but after spending some time in his company Tom decided that there was rather more to him than he had thought. (*Journal*, 22 January 1827)

wives' – was delayed for a few days. She arrived, fittingly enough, on Waterloo Day 1827, which was being celebrated by a dinner for all those officers who had been present at the battle.[39]

The Montagus' first child was born in the following year, just as the Regiment was about to return to England; it could hardly have been more precisely timed to match the surrounding chaos.[40]

~~~~

Tom sailed for Portugal on the *Wellesley*, with none other than Rear Admiral Sir Thomas Hardy on board. The officers and crew, disappointed at not going straight home after a long voyage from South America, nevertheless did their best to make 600 soldiers feel welcome – how everyone fitted in is difficult to imagine. The wardroom was made over to the Guards officers to use as their cabin

HMS Wellesley *in her heyday. She eventually became a training ship and was destroyed during an air raid in 1940.*

but, hardly surprisingly, it was always full. And as they moved further south, Tom's berth in the cockpit became unbearably hot; escaping to the deck provided some relief, even though naval etiquette did not allow him the luxury of sitting down or being at ease.[41]

LISBON

After ten days of crowded living and occasional seasickness, the *Wellesley* anchored at the mouth of the river Tagus; on the next day they slowly worked their way upwind, and finally took their place with eight other British warships, moored off the main harbour of Lisbon.

The Guards were barracked on arrival at Belem, strategically placed about four miles downriver at a slight narrowing of the estuary. It had – and still has – its own distinct character, with exuberantly decorated late gothic architecture. However, even then Belem and Lisbon were beginning to merge as a result of infill: 'dirty, low little houses' along the 'roughest and dirtiest' pavement that Tom had ever seen.[42]

The route became all too familiar, as Tom spent much of a cold and wet early January traipsing into Lisbon and back, presenting introductions and equipping himself. Amongst his purchases were two mules, Fatima and Selim: Fatima turned out to be a very bad tempered and not long afterwards kicked Tom so badly that he was laid up for a couple of days. He was the fourth officer to have been incapacitated in that way, and there were more cases to come – including no less a person than Lieutenant General Sir William Henry Clinton, his divisional commander.[43] The advantage that mules had over horses in sure-footedness and suitability for Portuguese roads was often paid for in their personality and, needless to say, Tom had great difficulty in selling her.

In the meantime, Portuguese Government forces defeated a much larger body of rebels at Corouches, about 170 miles north of Lisbon.

Belem Tower, built at the beginning of the sixteenth century to defend the entrance to the Tagus. In Tom's day it was further from the land, which has gradually been reclaimed.

With Spanish encouragement and assistance, however, the rebels had managed to regroup in the far northeast of Portugal: there were even reports of a possible war with Spain and concern about their troops massing on the border. The British sent a brigade 20 miles north to Vila Franca, held a Grand Field Day to reassure the Portuguese, and the last two regiments joined them from Gibraltar.

Rumours of where the Guards might be going came and went, but until a strategy emerged there was still plenty of time for Tom to do a little sightseeing. Once the Field Day was over, Tom and two other officers headed off for Cintra,* an easy ride west from Lisbon.

---

* The modern spelling is Sintra. It is a UNESCO World Heritage site.

Its spectacular scenery and buildings to match were already familiar to travelling English romantics; William Beckford had lived there in the 1790s and some years later Lord Byron had also left his mark – figuratively and, as we shall see, quite literally.

Cintra was also notorious for its association with the Convention of 1808 whereby, to widespread British disgust, the defeated French were allowed to evacuate their troops. Tom and his friends made a point of visiting the house belonging to the Marquis of Marialva, where the Convention was said to have been signed.

That identification was almost certainly wrong. One version of events is that the Convention only got its name because the despatch which referred to it was sent from Cintra, and that it was actually signed in Lisbon; another is that the Convention was signed in the Palace of Queluz, just outside Cintra, which Tom clearly distinguishes from the rather more ordinary house that he visited.

Byron's description of the area is considerably more flowery than Tom's, but two lines in *Childe Harold* reflect the wisdom of the time and have perhaps lent it credence:

> *Convention is the dwarfish demon styled,*
> *That foil'd the knights in Marialva's dome.*[44]

Even if Tom had not read the poem, he was certainly familiar with Byron's name, which he found, as well as that of an earlier Guards officer, scratched onto the belfry of a Cintra convent. According to Tom, it was situated at the top of a hill with a Moorish castle; the castle still exists, but it has not been possible to locate the convent. Byron's graffiti was clearly famous in Tom's day, but has most probably disappeared.

BRITISH DEPLOYMENT

The rest of the British troops had arrived by the time that Tom returned to Lisbon, although their numbers were still small in terms of what they might be asked to do. Assuming that the capital would be key to any attempt to overthrow the Government, the apparent strategy was to hold the area extending about 120 miles northwards to the Mondego river, flowing to the west; for much of that distance, the Tagus would provide a natural barrier to any incursion from the east.

The infantry was divided into three brigades (see Appendix V). Broadly speaking, regiments from the 1st Brigade – who had already marched out – were to be stationed in the northern sector with their headquarters at Coimbra, commanding the Mondego;[45] the 2nd Brigade were ordered to the middle of the sector and the Guards Brigade would be at the southern end, not very far from Lisbon itself.

The Royal Navy, in the unlikely event of a threat from the sea, could patrol much of the Tagus and also defend the capital. The British also had four squadrons of cavalry, whose actual role is unclear. Apart from their obvious role in a pitched battle, they could have mounted patrols, but from the little information that can be found this does not seem to have been among their functions.[46]

The Guards had less distance to go than the other brigades and waited until the end of January to move.[47] Apart from field days and Cintra, Tom had not previously been outside the Lisbon area, and even though it started unpromisingly in torrential rain he rather enjoyed the journey north. Staying fairly close to the western bank of the Tagus, they passed to the extreme right of the Lines of Torres Vedras, made famous during Wellington's Peninsular campaign. This was well-trodden territory for the British army, as Tom already knew, but it came home to him when he found a house with another inscription on its walls – the names of British officers billeted there in 1810.

As they continued past neglected farm buildings in the deeply rural countryside, all the signs of a once prosperous economy were plainly to be seen; uninhabited and decaying houses told the same story in the towns. The officers' billets were not too bad, although the men – in Tom's own words – were wretchedly off. However, the locals were friendly, despite or perhaps thanks to the British troops who had passed through earlier; on Tom's second halt, at Villa Franca, they even extended their welcome to a parade in the streets with music and fireworks. Tom decided that he liked these people much more than those in Lisbon or Belem.[48]

With a day's march lost to bad weather, it took five days to reach Cartaxo, about 50 miles north of Lisbon. Brigade Headquarters were established there, but the town itself was scarcely more than a large village, offering little in the way of accommodation; Tom was billeting officer, which had its obvious compensations as well as hard work. However, the resulting effort and inconvenience was made up for by the countryside: the last eight miles of the march had been through heathland, dotted with umbrella pines and intersected by streams running down tiny valleys. The next day Tom and his friends explored the area more extensively when they went out shooting and came back with plenty for dinner; it was 'capital country to be quartered in' with nice dry ground, varied with orchards, vineyards, olive groves and firs. He continued his explorations as the weather began to improve; perhaps not surprisingly, given his father's interest in the subject, his journal often includes notes on the local botany and these entries reveal him as quite an observant and even fluent writer.

They were destined to stay in the area for the next three months. The early weeks were spent in establishing themselves, basic administration and some more serious tests of preparedness.

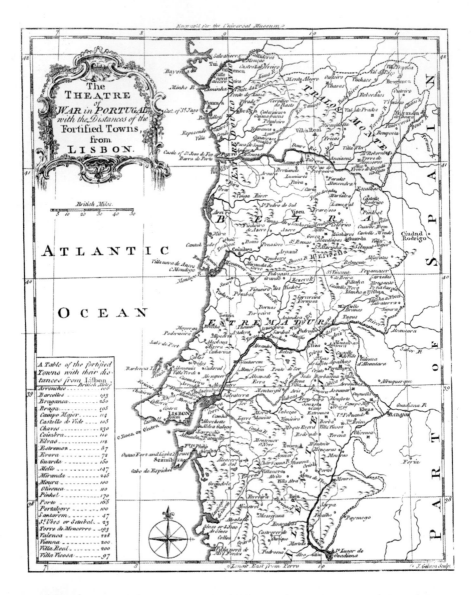

A map by John Gibson for the 'Universal Museum', an eighteenth-century periodical. The reference to 'The Theatre of War in Portugal' is to the Seven Years' War, towards the end of which an invasion by French and Spanish forces was repelled by an Anglo-Portuguese army. Little had changed when Tom was in Portugal sixty-four years later.

Militarily, Tom was getting quite senior and was obviously regarded as a safe pair of hands, for as well as his billeting duties he would often substitute for Montagu, who was Adjutant, and take the battalion out for drill.[49] Later they had field days, which he rather enjoyed, and on one occasion again stood in for Montagu; fortunately, the horse that he had bought after getting rid of Fatima turned out to be an excellent charger.[50] And when Montagu and his new bride finally managed to have a very delayed honeymoon at Cintra, he again obliged – but ironically spent most of that time laid up as a result of his horse stumbling on what passed for a Portuguese road.[51] Fatima may have been more sure-footed, but there is no indication at all that he regretted parting with her.

Being responsible for his men probably broadened Tom's outlook as well. There is a very touching account of a letter to one of them, sent by an unknowing widow after her husband had died. Tom wrote:

> I think we are very apt to underrate the affections and feelings of the lower classes. One of the most tender and affectionate letters I ever saw in my life came last post for a man in my company who died since our arrival in this country from his wife who was left at home. Poor creature, I am afraid she is little aware of the blow that awaits her.[52]

It is also interesting to note his slight surprise at the widespread desire of the men to write and receive letters from home.[53] Apart from anything else, it implies a certain degree of literacy, which we would possibly not have associated with soldiers of that period: one study estimates the literacy rate in the first half of the nineteenth century as about one-third, weighted towards the NCOs, who had to be able to read and write in order to function militarily.[54] Tom does not say who actually wrote and read these letters, however, and it is quite possible that an illiterate soldier could have asked a better-educated comrade to help him out.

—∿∿—

As tension gradually subsided, it allowed life to move towards more social enjoyment. The Portuguese may not have been very prosperous, but they knew how to enjoy themselves, either at festivals on Saints' Days – which seem to have been quite frequent – or at more secular and rather rustic race meetings. The weather also started to improve, and was often quite hot, with occasional violent showers; together these had a wonderful effect on the vegetation.

In the meantime, Portuguese Government troops had succeeded in pushing back the rebels, who fled north towards the Spanish frontier.[55] After a few days of skirmishing and manoeuvring, the rebels broke up and sought refuge in Spain, where they were accepted by the authorities who somewhat reluctantly made them lay down their arms and marched them into the interior. Others, who had been captured by Government forces, passed Tom on their way to Lisbon and an uncertain future. Some were well dressed, but apart from a fat priest on a donkey the majority were clearly peasants. Perhaps predictably, Tom was rather suspicious of any involvement of the Roman Catholic church: two days later there was news of desertions from the 1st Brigade, which he put down to priests at work amongst the Catholics of the 60th Rifles.[56]

The immediate crisis thus passed off, and although the British had hardly been involved the show of support had most probably helped to tip the balance.* The Guards marched back to Lisbon and were

---

* The *History of the Tenth Foot* (1911 edition) implies that British troops were actually involved in the fighting. This is most probably a garbled account of the actions of Portuguese Government forces, and support for it seems to be entirely lacking.

inspected by the Brigade Commander, Sir Henry Bouverie, who congratulated them on their good behaviour and – no doubt just as importantly to some – excused all punishments.

They were also much more lucky than the other regiments. The weather had begun to get extremely hot and even when the Guards returned at the end of April, they had needed to make an unplanned halt at Santarem because the men were too exhausted to carry on.* Other regiments stayed behind in the field. The 43rd Regiment remained at Thomar, about 80 miles north of Lisbon; when they came back in late July, they suffered badly from heatstroke and many men actually died.[57] The 11th Regiment, who marched with them, told a similar story: even though they had started at 2 o'clock in the morning, no more than the strength of a single company, taking both regiments together, was able to reach the convent at Santarem where they were to be quartered on the first day.[58]

LISBON LIFE

Keeping fit

Even the comparatively easy march that the Guards had undertaken confirmed Tom in his view that keeping fit was essential to well-being in the Portuguese climate. Once he had re-established himself in Lisbon, he made a practice of going out for long walks, which extended later to some lengthy expeditions on the back of a mule.

It also became possible to organise more systematic forms of exercise and entertainment. The steamer that had brought out Mrs Montagu also carried a six-oared boat belonging to the 3rd Guards.

---

* Later in his Journal, Tom mentions that his men had 60 lbs weight on their backs, and that they could hardly hold out during three hour drills in the heat of summer. (*Journal*, 2 July 1827)

Tom brought it ashore and took pleasure in rowing on the Tagus, with the double advantage of keeping himself fit and of benefiting from a cooling breeze. He was not alone in enjoying this pursuit – from taking Sir Henry and Lady Bouverie for a leisurely and no doubt diplomatically advantageous scull on the river[59] to an occasion when the Guards were challenged to a boat race by the Royal Navy.

That was serious business. The Guards were pitted against a crew of professional watermen from Cork and few, including Tom, gave much for the army's chances; this despondency increased just after the start of the race, when he broke his oar. However, they managed to pick up a spare about a quarter of the way in, overhauled the navy and actually won. This made such an impression that it was reported in the British press, in an article which thoughtfully noted the schools which the Guards crew had attended; three of the boat had been to Westminster and two to Eton.[60] Tom Wedgwood's schooldays had not been entirely wasted.

Those who were not oarsmen played cricket, or at least they watched it. Both Tom and that same press report mention a match between the Brigade of Guards and the Second Brigade of the Army. The Guards won convincingly, being much assisted by the performance of a young Ensign, Sir Frederick Hervey-Bathurst, who did rather well and went on to become the foremost cricketer of his day and the forebear of a long line of distinguished cricketers.

Relaxation

There was time and opportunity for less physical relaxation as well. Quite often, Tom would go to the opera after dinner; fortunately, a number of boxes had been taken by the Guards and he could usually get a seat rather than putting up with the pit, which tended to be quite rowdy. Rossini was popular and it is rather nice to think of him seeing *La Cenerentola* only ten years after it was written, or *Semiramide*,

The Lisbon Opera House, as it is today. The Guards established a club for themselves in a building which faced it from across the square.

which was even more recent; but works by other composers mentioned by Tom have largely disappeared into the mists of time and are hardly to be found, even in the best reference books. The performances themselves were probably not of the standard we would expect today, and on one occasion they actually had to do without the prima donna who had, as Tom explained, 'levanted'* that morning.

Besides its social function, the opera house acted as an unofficial forum for political and state purposes. The presence, or absence, of the Infanta at a performance was taken to have a deeper meaning, and as the situation grew more polarised towards the end of Tom's stay, interruptions or even speeches from the audience became quite frequent.

---

* That is, left suddenly without paying her debts.

Religion, Church and conscience

It was a religious age; Tom's Journal shows him to be roughly what one would have expected of the time, although there was perhaps an element of patriotism involved as well. He went to church on Sundays, taking comfort from the familiar form of service and satisfaction from the fact that an English church had, after a long dispute with the Inquisition, finally been built in Lisbon; it was such a contrast with the Roman Catholic 'mummeries' going on elsewhere.[61] However, he was equally capable of admiring the products of Catholic religious art, even when it was expressed in their church architecture.

Whether Tom shared in his mother's Evangelicalism and if so, how far, is more difficult to say. He was possibly more observant than some of his contemporaries and certainly disapproved of the sometimes poor attendance at the English church – not to mention feeling a momentary pang of conscience at the thought of playing cards on a Sunday.* Fortunately, this was mollified because he was not playing for money, but merely to entertain some young Portuguese ladies of his acquaintance, who obviously did not share his scruples.[62]

Tom was also pleased when the British authorities sent out extra chaplains to cater for the spiritual needs of the troops. Unfortunately their ship was wrecked – the third transport to suffer that fate – and initial rumours were that five chaplains had been on board and that three had been drowned. This turned out later to be an exaggeration on both counts; only two chaplains had been sent, and both had survived, although one of them had lost his wife.[63]

---

* His uncle, Jos Wedgwood, took a more relaxed view. When Bessy expressed uneasiness about having played cards on Sunday, he replied that 'as you do not think it wrong to do so, why should you object to Caroline [Drewe] or Jane knowing that you did? I am rather afraid of Evangelicalism spreading amongst us....' (*CFL* 1904 Vol. 1, p. 224)

British political developments

Meanwhile, the political situation at home had been getting more troublesome. Lord Liverpool, Prime Minister for nearly fifteen years, had a stroke and resigned at the beginning of April 1827. He was succeeded by Canning, who was deserted by the right wing of the Tory party and held office for only four months; to be fair, he was in bad health at the time, having caught a severe cold at the Duke of York's funeral in early January. However, his successor, Lord Goderich, managed to last as Prime Minister for only three days longer than he did.

Foreign affairs were also a problem. The Greek War of Independence had been going on for about five years and the Great Powers sensed that Turkey, while not quite yet terminally ill, was in a vulnerable condition; the carefully contrived balance of power was thus in danger of falling apart. Britain, in particular, was concerned about Russian expansionism, although Wellington had obtained a degree of comfort when he visited the new Tsar, Nicholas I,* in early 1826.[64]

This optimism was extinguished a year or so later by the Battle of Navarino, in which the entire Turkish fleet was annihilated by the British, French and Russians. It was widely applauded by the general public, possibly reflecting support for Greek independence, but more likely in some cases because they thought it time for another crushing naval victory; pubs were named after Admiral Codrington, who had commanded the fleet. George IV shared the popular sentiment – and even knighted Codrington – until he was put right by the politicians, who were aghast: diplomatically they referred to it as 'an

---

* Nicholas I turned out to have all the reactionary qualities associated with the Romanovs; his expansionist policies led directly to the Crimean war, but by then Tom had left the army. Montagu (as Lord Rokeby) was still serving and took command of the Guards Brigade in February 1855. He was said to have been moved to tears when he saw the haggard faces of the few officers who still remained effective. (*ODNB*)

untoward event', which seems in fact to have occurred as the result of misunderstandings and poor communication.

Whatever the cause, it was the last straw for Goderich's ministry. He resigned in January 1828 and his successor was none other than the Duke of Wellington, who had spent the previous eight years doing an extremely good job as Master General of the Ordnance. That was a Cabinet position, but matched his skills exactly: being Prime Minister was rather different, and depended on being able to reach a workable compromise. It is said that after his first Cabinet meeting in that role, he remarked that it had been 'an extraordinary affair; I gave them their orders and they wanted to stay and discuss them'. This may or may not be apocryphal, but it has a ring of truth.[65]

There is little doubt, however, that he brought to that position an extremely quick mind and a strong sense of realism. Even though his analysis might result in a solution that he would not ideally have desired, he seems to have recognised that politics – then and as now – were the art of the possible. His eventual acceptance of Catholic Emancipation is, perhaps, an example of this.

More immediately, one might also have thought that he would take a particular interest in Portuguese affairs. However, Portugal was geopolitically a sideshow and in the wake of Navarino attention had begun to focus on the eastern Mediterranean.*

The British withdrawal

In Portugal itself, the Spanish threat appeared to have receded and thus removed the Canningite justification for a British presence. Dom Miguel, a potential claimant to the throne, had been released from

---

* When the British army left Portugal six months later, two of the regiments were posted to the Ionian Islands. These had never been part of the Ottoman Empire and had become a British Protectorate in the aftermath of Waterloo.

exile and was already in England, having arrived at the end of 1827. He had created a moderately favourable impression and, on the basis that he would uphold the Constitution and support the monarchy as it had been settled, the new Cabinet agreed to withdraw the British force and Miguel sailed for Portugal. Perhaps there were some individual but unvoiced reservations, but even if the worst suspicions were confirmed – which they very soon were – 5,000 troops would not be able to influence matters in a full-scale civil war.

Rumours of a return to England were already circulating amongst the British troops in Portugal and this was visibly confirmed when transports began to arrive towards the end of February.[66] Miguel, who had arrived in Lisbon a few days earlier, swore to uphold the Constitution and was installed as lieutenant general to his brother; his sincerity is scarcely believable, but the Queen Mother was certainly having none of this and ensured that he appointed a ministry of carefully selected absolutists.[67]

Even before Miguel's arrival the atmosphere in Lisbon had begun to get tense, with a more obvious division between the opposing factions of Portuguese society. Tom – and his men – were firmly on the side of the Constitutionalists, and Tom had no illusions about the likely course of events when they left, describing Miguel as a rascal.[68] The men felt the same, and rather enjoyed it when their band played the *Constitutional Air* to demonstrate that fact.* In the end such musical teasing was forbidden by their divisional commander, Lieutenant General Sir William Henry Clinton, who was obviously reluctant to stir things up still further.[69]

---

* The *Constitutional Air* (or *Hymn of the Charter*) is a rather jolly tune that would have sounded well when played by a military band of fifes and drums. It was officially proclaimed as the Portuguese National Anthem in 1834 but was replaced in 1910.

The final weeks of the British presence make sad reading. Their imminent departure emboldened the Absolutists; two of the best regiments in the Portuguese army were sent out of town and dispersed; and Miguel made little pretence of Constitutional rule. The Constitutionalists felt that the British had raised their hopes and then left them to their fate, a reproach that Tom thought well merited. His only satisfaction was one Sunday, when Miguel had taken to the river and became enraged because the British Fleet did not salute him: he was later informed by the Admiral that they were at Divine Service and could not be interrupted.[70]

The British could get away with being rude to Miguel, but those Portuguese inclined to the Constitution had a much harder time. As the date of the British departure drew more close, Tom was approached by people desperate to leave; he thought they had been badly let down, but was obviously unable to help. The final passage in his Journal records the farewell to a small girl who had been 'adopted' by a man in his company and had since become his protégée: she had no father and an old, infirm mother who was hopelessly poor. After a long day in the barracks he found her waiting outside and gave her some small coins, whereupon she seized his hand and without a word pressed it to her heart.[71]

Towards the end of April, when the British had left and Miguel had begun to show his true colours, Palmerston (at that point Secretary at War) summed things up. He wrote privately:

Miguel seems to be going to the devil as fast as he can.... It is provoking, but we cannot help it. Our troops did not go to interfere in the affairs of Portugal, or to dictate a government to the Nation…. If they like an absolute king and an usurper it is their own affair, and if they don't, they ought to say so, and to resist.[72]

The resulting civil war dragged on until the middle of 1834, when Miguel renounced his claim to the throne and went into exile for good. Dom Pedro restored the Constitution and Maria, by then fifteen years old, resumed her role as Queen.

TOM'S LATER YEARS

RETURN TO ENGLAND AND MARRIAGE

Tension and weak government were still dogging political life when Tom returned to England, but by and large disturbances during the years leading up to the Great Reform Act of 1832 took place outside London and the Guards do not seem to have been seriously involved. We have little insight into Tom's military duties, although he had been promoted – again by purchase – to Captain & Lieutenant Colonel at the end of 1830.

In the meantime the John Wedgwoods had become, in Henrietta Litchfield's words, 'a much-wandering family'. The collapse of Davison's bank in 1816 accelerated a process which had been going on for more than a decade, and they moved regularly as circumstances of economy and family ties demanded. During Tom's absence in Portugal they had left their most recent home, Kingscote Cottage, near Tetbury, and seem to have spent a year or so in Europe. By 1830 they were settled for the time being at The Hill, in Abergavenny, which marked the start of a move closer to Pembroke and the Allen family home.*

We catch a few glimpses of Tom in family letters, especially those of the Darwin sisters, who kept Charles up to date with the gossip while he was away on the *Beagle*. From these meagre sources, Tom

---

* Kingscote Cottage was the Dower House to Kingscote Park, and by no means small. The Big House was demolished in 1951 and the Cottage is now known as Kingscote Park House. The Hill was – and still is – a fairly large eighteenth-century house, recently used as a college of further education. It is now being converted into apartments and modern houses have been built in the grounds – renamed Wedgwood Country Park.

comes across as an agreeable young man; there is even a hint of unreciprocated romance in one of Susan Darwin's letters, written in November 1832.[73]

> I have been spending a very gay Autumn. October at the Hill was very delightful. Tom and Robert* were both there & both Masters of Gigs so with the Phaeton we had no ends of pretty drives and exploring parties. Also a family of Michells live close there & joined in our excursions. Miss Michell is rather good looking and very lively. We always used to set her down as Tom's Lady but now I have seen them together I see no symptoms on Tom's side.
>
> Capt Michell her brother was very pleasant & a famous Sportsman. When we made parties by the river side he used to catch trout for our Dinner & cook them over a Stove which belonged to Tom on his Portuguese service.

John and Jenny left The Hill three or four years later, intending to return to Staffordshire, but Jenny was taken seriously ill. She died suddenly in April 1836, while visiting Shrewsbury in order to take medical advice from Robert Darwin.[74]

Tom had just got engaged and his mother's death affected him deeply. A few days afterwards, Fanny Allen wrote to her cousin, Emma Wedgwood:

> I feel very sorry for the shock poor Tom will have felt at Clifton; his state of mind was so happy, that sorrow is doubly felt under its influence. I think his marriage with Anne Tyler promises as much happiness as is ever likely to fall to the share of anyone,

---

* Tom's younger brother, who was also unmarried at the time – see Biographical Notes in Appendix I.

Admiral Sir Charles Tyler

weighing all matters fairly. Anne has a most sweet and gentle nature as well as temper, a most ardent affection for him and all his family, and is as liberal as daylight.[75]

Tom's fiancée was the daughter of Admiral Sir Charles Tyler, who had been one of Nelson's captains at Trafalgar, and the Tylers were family friends.* Fanny's slightly reserved comment about Tom and Anne's future happiness was probably a reference to their ages –

---

* The then Captain Tyler was wounded at Trafalgar and had returned to Spithead, whereupon Jos wrote to him suggesting that instead of going back to Pembroke to recover, he might prefer to stay at Gunville, where Jos and Bessy were living at the time. Gunville is in Dorset, so he could have travelled to Poole or Southampton by sea and then taken the road, which would have been a much shorter and easier journey. Jos added that Bessy was a 'good nurse, who would do her best to recruit you'; the letter could well have been written at her instigation, but the offer was probably not taken up. (*Windham-Quinn*, pp. 154-5)

Tom was in his late thirties, and Anne was almost eight years older. We do not know whether she was the young lady who is said to been recommended by Hensleigh Wedgwood as a possible bride and in possession of £500 a year, but whose name he could not remember![76]

Tom was not the only one grieving, however. Anne's mother had also died quite recently, and she had been followed shortly afterwards by her husband. At the very least these events must have cast a further shadow over the wedding, five months after Jenny's death; it took place at Boulston,[77] quite close to the Allen family home at Cresselly.

Despite the proximity, Boulston was not an obvious place for Tom and Anne to get married. There was, however, a connection because Anne's sister Caroline had married the local landowner, Robert Ackland. The most likely explanation is that Anne had been living with the Acklands,[78] although the reason for this and whether it was a long-term arrangement are not clear. Tom, on the other side, probably had no separate household of his own and simply spent his leaves with relations (the letter to Siborne would be consistent with this) but it does not really explain the choice of Boulston: one would expect the bride's immediate family to have had greater involvement.

A possible explanation is provided by the Tylers' domestic circumstances. For the last twenty years the family home had been Cottrell House, in Glamorgan. After Admiral Tyler's death it had been taken over by his second son, who had a very large and very young family. It is not difficult to imagine that living space might have been rather limited, and could have accounted for Anne's presence at Boulston, although we have nothing positive to confirm this.

About a year after they were married, Tom retired from the army and set up house with Anne at Portclew, a small hamlet near the coastal village of Freshwater East.[79]

JOHN WEDGWOOD OF BIGNALL END

Josiah Clement Wedgwood (Josiah IV) tells a rather unfortunate story about Tom. John Wedgwood of Bignall End in Staffordshire – a first cousin of Sarah Wedgwood, Tom's grandmother – had intended to make Tom his heir. He had a large estate, with wealth derived from coalmines; he died in 1839 and was commemorated by a large obelisk on Bignall Hill. It is still there, although most of it was blown down by a storm in 1976.

About a year before he died, and shortly after Tom and Anne were married, he wrote a will in which most of his estate would pass to John for his life and then to Tom. Scarcely more than a month later, he revoked it without naming an heir. Josiah IV's version of events in *Wedgwood Pedigrees* is essentially that Tom snubbed his prospective benefactor, being unaware of his intended generosity and too grand to deal with him on equal terms.[80]

This tale may well be true, but must be set against Josiah's firm conviction that Wedgwoods should not adopt airs and graces. The version of events in his earlier *History of the Wedgwood Family* does not include an explanation, although his narrative is so amusing that it deserves to be quoted in full:

> *Shortly before his death however [John Wedgwood] cancelled this rather strange succession and left his estates to trustees 'to be hereafter named'. They were never named, with the result that after many years the estates were divided between the Woods and the Yeeles [the families by marriage of his two nieces, but also distant cousins, at least in the case of the Woods] as heirs general. For some wonderful reason however the idea spread among all the wider ramifications of the Wedgwood clan that the 'Government' were looking for the lineal male heir of John*

The memorial to John Wedgwood of Bignall End.

Wedgwood of Bignall End in order to make over to the happy claimant the vast wealth of this mysterious millionaire. The estates were never entailed; they had only been bought as we have seen in the previous generation. That did not matter however. The Newspapers magnified the prize, and every man who spelt his name Wedgwood began tracing his pedigree. Curiously enough the Wedgwoods of Yorkshire, who cannot even connect on with Staffordshire, have fought the hardest for the reversion. Companies have been formed to divide the spoil, and have been spoiled in turn by the lawyers. Mr James Wedgwood, farrier and practical shoeing smith of York, has spent the last 50 years of his life in vain efforts and wonderful researches.[81]

He added, more practically, that this dispute had been of great value in his genealogical work.

A possible, and in some ways just as plausible, explanation is hinted at in a letter from Emma Darwin. Shortly after John Wedgwood of Bignall End had died, she wrote to her sister, Charlotte Langton:[82]

Ellen was talking to me about old Mr Wedgwood. She fully believes that it was Mr Harding's tattling which did the mischief.

Ellen is clearly Ellen Tollet, who was an old childhood friend.* The identification of 'Mr Harding' is less certain, but Emma may well have been referring to the vicar of St George's Shrewsbury, which the Darwins attended.[83] Whoever he was, however, there is a clear implication that he was rather a gossip.

---

* The Tollets owned an estate a few miles from the Jos Wedgwoods' home in Maer, and when Davison's bank collapsed they had let a cottage to John and his family on favourable terms.

What was actually said and by whom is obviously crucial: on the conventional reading Tom had made derogatory remarks about John Wedgwood of Bignall End and these reached his ears.

There is little doubt that John Wedgwood of Bignall End was a difficult man: at the age of sixty-five he had been sued by a widow for breach of promise, and lost.[84] And he was not above bringing somewhat doubtful litigation himself, where it suited his business ends.[85] It could simply be that he was averse to 'tattling', especially about his private affairs.

Whatever the true reason may have been, Emma then goes on to say of Tom's family that:

One of their castles in the air was building a nice parsonage for Allen, which would have been money well employed by way of getting him a wife too. If Tom had got the estate, it would have given Miss Charlotte Yea a pang I think.[86]

Both the context and full meaning of the last sentence are unclear. However, from the way in which Emma puts it, Tom seems to have had some hopes of marrying a Miss Charlotte Yea and was rebuffed for lack of money.

This is even more speculative than the identification of Mr Harding, but the Yeas (or Yeos) were prominent in the West Country and could well have been known to Tom's family. There are indeed records of a Miss Charlotte Yea, born in 1795, who eventually married a Robert Grant in 1820 – but it would be unfair, even now, to take these conjectures any further.[87]

TENBY

After some years at Portclew, Tom and Anne settled in Tenby, a pretty little town on the Pembrokeshire coast, which was already a promising seaside resort.[88] In due course, it also became the home of various Allen aunts. The widowed Jessie Sismondi and the unmarried Emma and Fanny Allen settled there over the next few years and made their final move in early 1850, where they shared a house in Heywood Lane, near to Tom and Anne who lived at St Mary's.[89] Jessie offers a small insight into their household in a letter written to her niece Elizabeth Wedgwood at the end of March that year:

> *We are obliged to build a room after all, for Mr Williams was right, we had not so much as we had in the other house. I shall long for your seeing it as soon as we are finished, and I think you will seldom have seen a nicer, prettier, more cheerful dwelling.… From the first moment I knew it could not take less than £200, and I have it ready, and it is so pleasant a way of spending we shall not much care if it comes to 3, but Tom says £200 will do it amply, so do not be alarmed for us…. Here is a pretty second winter for you! Anne gave us most excellent pancakes from the snow and flour only, neither eggs nor milk. I hope you tried them, they would have consoled you for the snow. She and Tom do not seem to tire of us, and our only danger is, of being to sorry to leave….*[90]

Tom had rapidly become part of the local establishment, being appointed a Justice of the Peace almost as soon as he arrived.[91] To this he added committee membership of the Tenby National School, the Royal National Lifeboat Society (where he was local chairman), treasurer of the local branch of the Society for the Propagation of the

Gospel, and also Town Councillor. All in all, he was clearly regarded as suitable material.[92]

Outside these good works, Tom made friends with another recent arrival, Dr Frederick Dyster, who was not only a practising doctor, attending to Jessie Sismondi when she died, but also a man with a lively mind. One of his interests was natural history, as a result of which he also became friendly with Thomas Henry Huxley, who had been sent on a survey of fish stocks in Carmarthen Bay. Dear to the hearts of both Dyster and Huxley was workers' education: Huxley lectured on 'Natural History and how to study it' – while he was actually on his honeymoon in Tenby – and Dyster lectured on subjects such as 'Nutrition and Physiology of Digestion', given to the gloriously named *Young Men's Mutual Improvement Association*.[93]

Quite when Dyster became acquainted with Tom is unclear. Tom's interest in botany, which we noted in his Portuguese days, was possibly the spark that started their friendship, although the fact that Charles Darwin was Tom's first cousin may not have escaped Dyster's attention. In any event, it is clear that he had a high regard for Tom.

Anne died in September 1855, at the age of sixty-six. From this time onwards, we hear very little of Tom apart from references to his public roles. What we do know is that he followed her five years later, at the relatively young age of sixty-two, and was buried with her in the churchyard of St Mary's, Tenby.* No reference to the circumstances of his death has been found: like the good soldier that he was, he seems simply to have faded away.

---

* Wedgwood Pedigrees suggests that they had two infants who died young, but it seems highly unlikely and the author has found nothing to confirm this.

However, he was not forgotten by his friend Frederick Dyster, who erected a public fountain in his honour. It originally stood in front of St Mary's church and for some years was rather neglected, but has recently been restored and moved to a new site in Tudor Square. A plaque on the fountain reads:

THIS FOUNTAIN WAS GIVEN BY DR DYSTER

IN MEMORY OF

LIEUT COL THOMAS WEDGWOOD

3RD GUARDS OF ST MARY'S HILL TENBY

WHO DIED NOV 7TH 1860, AGED 62

HE FOUGHT AT WATERLOO

'Dyster's fountain' in Tenby, from an old postcard

APPENDICES

APPENDIX I

All website addresses were correct at the time of printing

BIOGRAPHICAL NOTES – THE WEDGWOOD AND ALLEN FAMILIES

The Wedgwood and Darwin sides have been studied extensively, but the Allens are less well known. They were landed gentry, and the key figure in subsequent Wedgwood relationships is John Bartlett Allen (1733–1803) who had an estate at Cresselly, in Pembrokeshire. He had twelve surviving children by his first wife, but when she died he took up with and married a coal miner's daughter, with whom he had further children and a separate household, but forbade any social contact between the families.

A very useful guide to the Allens of Cresselly can be found online. However, it is probably based on Burke's Landed Gentry, which tends to ignore cadet branches, and is not as complete as may appear at first sight. It can be found at:

http://landedfamilies.blogspot.com/2014/01/102-allen-families-of-pembrokeshire.html

There is also a very illuminating paper, *A Pembrokeshire County Family in the Eighteenth Century* by Elizabeth Inglis-Jones, which describes the Wedgwood and Allen relationship over a period of fifty years. While much of it is familiar from *A Century of Family Letters*, there are many details that must have come from other primary sources – possibly from Allen family papers. Unfortunately, it contains virtually no information on such matters.

The paper was published in three parts, the first of which starts when the Wedgwoods and Allens first met and ends in about 1814. This part is available on the web and can be found at:

http://www.genuki.org.uk/big/wal/PEM/Jeffreyston/Allen.html

Tom's immediate family

Tom's father was **John Wedgwood** (1766–1844), the eldest son of Josiah Wedgwood I and chiefly remembered as a founder of the Royal Horticultural Society. He died during a visit to Tenby and was buried at St Mary's Church, which contains his memorial.[94]

Tom's mother was **Louisa Jane Allen** (1771–1836), known as Jane or Jenny. Despite always seeming younger than her years, Jenny died at the age of sixty-five, while visiting the Darwins in Shrewsbury. Robert Darwin was still alive at that point, although his wife Susannah (John's elder sister) had died nearly twenty years previously.

John and Louisa had seven children, of whom Tom was the third. They were:

> **Sarah Elizabeth Wedgwood** (1795–1857), known generally as Eliza, if only to distinguish her from Josiah II's eldest daughter, who had the same names and was much the same age. She was an invalid, described by Henrietta Litchfield as a 'fading flower', but who nevertheless managed to live to the age of sixty-two. She was unmarried.

John Allen Wedgwood (1796–1882), known as Allen. After a rather aimless childhood, he became Perpetual Curate* of Maer through the patronage of his uncle, Josiah II. He officiated at the marriage of Charles Darwin to Josiah's daughter, Emma Wedgwood, tempering the Anglican service to her Unitarian beliefs. He retired in about 1864 and Emma's daughter, Henrietta Litchfield, described him thus: 'He died over 86 years of age, having spent a long life largely occupied in taking care of his health, for he remained an invalid. He had a kindly and simple nature, and, like his father, was devoted to flowers and gardening'.[95] He was unmarried.

Thomas Josiah Wedgwood (1797–1860), the subject of this work. Married to Anne Maria Tyler in 1836. She died in 1855.

Caroline Louisa Jane Wedgwood (1799–1825), unmarried and died of consumption in her mid-twenties.

Charles Wedgwood (1800–20), an 'undisciplined and adventurous young man' according to *The Wedgwood Circle*. The basis for this is unclear, but he does seem to have taken some time to settle down to a career. Despite the reference to Woolwich in Tom's letter, he finally became a Cadet in the East India Company's service. He arrived in India in June 1820 and three months later he was dead; it took another six months for notice of his death to appear in the English press.

---

* An obsolete form of incumbency, essentially that of a vicar with a cash stipend instead of ancient rights to glebe or tithe.

Like his sister Caroline, he had been diagnosed as consumptive by Robert Darwin, although his death was said to be 'the result of a fever' – in those days more than likely in India. He was unmarried.

Jessie Wedgwood (1804–72) married Jos's second son, Henry Allen Wedgwood, in 1830. He qualified as a barrister, although he seems not to have practised very much. He was the author of a rather charming children's book, *The Bird Talisman*, which was reprinted in 1939 with illustrations by his great-niece, Gwen Raverat.

Jessie and Henry had six children. One of these, John Darwin Wedgwood, married Helen Margaret Tyler, the niece of Tom's wife Anne, in 1866.

Robert Wedgwood (1806–81), who like his brother Allen, went into the Church but had to wait a long time before finding a permanent living. Robert held sporadic curacies during his early career, and there were several years without a formal position; at one point he assisted his brother at Maer. He seems to have been curate of Woking from 1847– 50,[96] which may possibly have been facilitated by his cousin Henry Wedgwood (see Jessie Wedgwood, above) who had recently moved there. In 1851 he finally became Rector of Dumbleton, Gloucestershire – again through patronage, this time through the Willett family, one of whom had married Josiah I's sister.

In 1834 he married Frances Crewe, the daughter of the vicar for whom he was acting as curate, but she died without children in 1845. Two years later he married Mary Halsey, whose family owned Henley Park in Surrey. They had seven children, of whom five – all of them daughters – survived into adulthood; only three of these daughters married, two of them to Allen cousins.

Mary appears to have been a rather formidable woman, at least judging by her portrait by John Singer Sargent, which hangs in the Wedgwood Museum. Her unmarried daughters had formidable reputations as well. The elder of the two, Henrietta, became Matron of the Royal Free Hospital. Her younger sister, Eliza, ran a VAD hospital in Winchcombe during World War I, a few miles away from Dumbleton. She was known locally as 'The Queen of Stanton' and a watercolour of her, also by Sargent, is in the Tate Gallery.

Other children of John Bartlett Allen

Elizabeth Allen: (1764–1836): known as Bessy and married to John's brother, Josiah II.

Catherine Allen (1765–1830): married to Sir James Mackintosh, a Whig lawyer, writer and politician. There was some hope that he would be asked to join Canning's Cabinet in 1827, but this did not happen[97] and he died in 1832. One of their daughters, Frances, married Josiah II's son Hensleigh Wedgwood – see below.

Caroline Allen (1768–1835): married to the Rev Edward Drewe, who died in 1810, leaving her with seven children to look after. See also Francis Fownes-Luttrell in Appendix II.

John Hensleigh Allen (1769–1843): brother of Jenny and Bessy. He was affable and very well regarded, and later became MP for Pembroke (Town). He inherited Cresselly in 1803 and married Gertrude Seymour in 1812, at which point his unmarried sisters left the house and went to live with relatives. His wife died in 1825 – like Caroline Wedgwood of consumption, while under the treatment of Dr Baron – and his sisters Emma and Fanny Allen then returned to Cresselly.[98]

Lancelot Baugh Allen (1774–1845): known as Baugh. He married, first, Caroline Jane Romilly in 1820, with whom he had two sons, and secondly, Georgina Sarah Bayly in 1841, with whom he had two sons and a daughter. Caroline Romilly was the niece of Sir Samuel Romilly, a prominent reformist lawyer of Huguenot descent. He was within the same circle as Sir James Mackintosh – see Catherine Allen, above – and Jean Charles de Sismondi, who married Jessie Allen, below.

Harriet Allen (1776–1845): married to the Rev. Matthew Surtees, Rector of North Cerney in Gloucestershire. From Harriet's point of view, this marriage – to a vicar twenty years her senior – was an escape, but she seems to have jumped out of the frying pan into the fire: even Bessy had been unable to hide her disapproval of the match. See also James Allen, below.

Jessie Allen (1777–1853): married to Jean Charles de Sismondi, a Swiss historian and political economist – see Lancelot Baugh Allen, above. In her final years she shared a house in Tenby with her younger sisters Emma and Fanny, not far from the house in which Tom and Anne also lived.

Emma Allen (1780–1866): unmarried – see Jessie Allen, above.

Frances (Fanny) Allen (1781–1875): unmarried – see Jessie Allen, above.

Cousins

The Wedgwood/Allen/Darwin 'cousinage' was extremely wide and only those referred to in this work are mentioned here.

John Wedgwood's generation

Robert Darwin (1766–1848): a doctor and also a shrewd financier. Son of Erasmus Darwin, a friend of Josiah I and fellow member of the Lunar Society, an informal group of prominent figures in the Midlands Enlightenment. Married to John's eldest sister Susannah.

Jos Wedgwood (1769–1843): John's younger brother, married to Bessy Allen, Jenny's sister. Sometimes known as Josiah Wedgwood II. After the death of his father, the pottery works went through a rather troubled period but in 1805 he resumed active management and eventually held it all together.

Tom Wedgwood's generation

Charles Darwin (1809–82): son of Robert Darwin and John Wedgwood's eldest sister, Susannah. Married his first cousin, Emma Wedgwood, in 1839 – see below.

Susan Darwin (1803–66): third daughter of Robert and Susannah Darwin. Unmarried.

Charlotte Wedgwood (1797–1862): daughter of Jos and Bessy Wedgwood. Married the Rev. Charles Langton in 1832; Tom's brother Allen officiated at the wedding.

Emma Wedgwood (1808–96): youngest daughter of Jos and Bessy Wedgwood; married to Charles Darwin, above. Henrietta Litchfield, the author of *A Century of Family Letters,* was one of their daughters.

Hensleigh Wedgwood (1803–91): son of Jos and Bessy Wedgwood. For a time, he sat as a Police Magistrate in London, but eventually resigned on the grounds that the administration of oaths was against the New Testament. He is chiefly remembered as the author of an early dictionary of English etymology. He married his cousin Frances Mackintosh, the daughter of Catherine Allen – see above.

More distant relations

James Allen: probably the James Allen who was a son of Roger Allen, of Freestone Hall, a younger brother of John Bartlett Allen. He was the first cousin of Bessy and her sisters. According to Elisabeth Inglis-Jones, James opened a drapery shop in Cheapside, where Bessy took her sister Harriet to buy her wedding clothes.[99]

Tom Allen: probably the Thomas G. Allen who wrote to Baugh Allen in 1809; the letter is reproduced in *A Wedgwood at Waterloo*. It was written at sea just after the retreat from Corunna and is very interesting in its own right. A Thomas Griffith Allen is listed in various naval sources and was probably the same person: he died at Port Louis in 1814, shortly after assuming command of *HMS Harpy*. Audley refers to him as Baugh's paternal nephew, but there is no reference to him in the family tree.

The Ridgways: *The Waterloo Roll Call* lists 1st Lieut John Allen Ridgway, of the 2nd Battalion, 95th Regiment of Foot (Rifles), as having taken part the battle. He was wounded but eventually became a Lieutenant Colonel and died in 1856. From the name, it seems highly likely that he was an Allen relation, but the exact connection is unclear and no reference to the older Ridgway has been found elsewhere.

The link is rather tenuous, but fifteen years earlier Bessy Wedgwood had visited her father at Cresselly and written to Jos, mentioning that she had considered and rejected a scheme to gratify a 'Mary Allen' with an invitation and to take 'Mary Ridgway' into their house.[100] Jos replied that he would have had no objection to Mary Allen, except for the lack of space, but was rather dismissive of Mary Ridgway as a companion for their children, although that does not seem to have been Bessy's intention.* A footnote in the 1915 version of *A Century of Family Letters* explains that Bessy wished to bring back her cousin, Mary Allen, and also 'little Ridgway', because she was 'half starved'. Mary Allen was obviously related to Bessy, although the exact link in unknown, and it may be that the Ridgways were also related but had fallen on hard times.

Friends of the family

Mr Currey or **Dr Curriey**: Tom's letter of 14 August 1815 implies that these are different people, one of whom was in France and the other in England when the letter was written. Despite the variation in spelling, it seems likely that the surname is actually the same.

Lieutenant Colonel Edmund Currey was Secretary and Comptroller to the Duke of Gloucester, Colonel of the 3rd Foot Guards. A letter dated 11 January 1814, from him to one of the Allens (probably Baugh), is held by the Wedgwood Museum. In it he mentions the 'absolute necessity of Tom's joining the moment he is gazetted'. He also encourages Tom to keep up his studies.

Unless Edmund Currey's duties had taken him to France, it seems unlikely that Tom is referring to him. However, he had several brothers, one of whom served the Duke as Confidential Solicitor. This brother, Benjamin, may possibly be the person that Tom met.

---

* *A Century of Family Letters* (1915), p. 17.

Mr Horner: Francis Horner (1778–1817): born in Edinburgh and known to the family through Sir James Mackintosh, who had married Jenny's sister Catherine Allen. Horner was one of the founders of the *Edinburgh Review* and a Whig statesman who disapproved of the settlement achieved by the Congress of Vienna and the Bourbon restoration.

APPENDIX II

BIOGRAPHICAL NOTES – OFFICERS MENTIONED IN TOM'S LETTERS

Captain Ashton 'of my Company': Lieutenant & Captain John Ashton, 2/3rd Foot Guards. From an old Cheshire family; son of John Ashton and Mary Noble Jarrett. They were friends of the Duke of Gloucester, who personally broke the news of their son's death. There is some confusion here as MacKinnon lists Ashton as belonging to the Grenadier Company and Tom to the Fifth.[101] Tom is very unlikely to have been in the former. Tom also refers to Captain Canning (see below) as being 'of my company' and Canning is listed as being in the Fifth.

Sir John Byng: Major General Sir John Byng, commander of the 2nd Brigade of Guards, which comprised the 2nd Battalions of the Coldstreams and Tom's own regiment, the 3rd Foot Guards. He was related to Admiral Byng. After a distinguished military career, he took up politics and supported the Reform Bill, for which he was rewarded with a peerage as the 1st Earl of Strafford.

Canning 'of my Company': Captain & Lieutenant Colonel Charles Fox Canning, 3rd Foot Guards – ADC to the Duke of Wellington. Canning was elder brother to Stratford Canning, the diplomat and eventually 1st Viscount Stratford de Redcliffe, and was invited to the Duchess of Richmond's ball. He has a very splendid memorial in St Joseph's Church, Waterloo – and is also commemorated on a second memorial, which lists all the officers of the 3rd Foot Guards who died in the battle.

In Canning's absence by reason of his duties as ADC, command of the 5th Company passed to Lieutenant & Captain Fairfield, whom Tom does not mention.

Crawford (sic): Lieutenant & Captain Thomas Gregan Craufurd, 1st Company, 2/3rd Foot Guards. He was born in 1792, the eldest son of Sir James Gregan-Craufurd of Kilbirnie, 2nd Bt and Maria Theresa Gage. His remains are buried in the church at Hengrave, Suffolk.[102] His younger brother, Alexander Charles Craufurd, also fought at Waterloo as a volunteer in the 12th Light Dragoons.

Forbes: Lieutenant & Captain The Hon. Hastings Brudenell Forbes, 2/3rd Foot Guards. Third son of the 6th Earl Granard (an Irish title); born 5th December 1793. He was invited to the Richmond Ball, but whether he managed to attend is not known. He had fallen in love with a Belgian lady who had given him a miniature of herself to wear around his neck. A friend fulfilled his dying request to return the portrait, which was 'almost shivered to pieces'.[103]

Lieutenant Colonel Sir A. Gordon: Captain & Lieutenant Colonel The Hon. Sir Alexander Gordon KCB, 3rd Foot Guards – ADC to the Duke of Wellington (see also Canning, above). He was badly wounded while rallying the Brunswickers near La Haye Sainte, and is said to have died in Wellington's own camp bed during the night.

He was the brother of Lord Aberdeen, who later became Prime Minister.

Captain Luttrell: Lieutenant & Captain Francis Fownes-Luttrell, 1st Foot Guards. He was in the Light Company of the 2nd Battalion. The Light Companies of all four Guards Battalions were brigaded as a single unit under Lieutenant Colonel Lord Saltoun and involved in the defence of Hougoumont right from the start. He recovered from his wounds and left the service in 1825.

He was born in 1792 and was the 3rd son of John Fownes-Luttrell, of Dunster Castle and MP for Minehead. His mother was Mary Drewe, whose brother Edward had married Tom's aunt, Caroline Allen – see Appendix I. In 1824, Francis married his first cousin Emma Drewe, the daughter of his uncle Samuel. He died in 1862.

Lieutenant Colonel McDonall (sic): Captain & Lieutenant Colonel James Macdonell, commander of the Light Company, 2/Coldstream Guards and officer commanding all troops within the château of Hougoumont, which included the Light Company of Tom's own regiment. He was a powerfully built man and reputed to have been personally responsible for closing the gate. He afterwards became Field Marshal Sir James Macdonell.

He was the third son of Duncan Macdonell of Glengarry and died on 15 May 1857.

The Prince of Orange: Commander of I Corps. Brought up in England and entered the British Army. He returned to the Netherlands in 1813. He was popular and courageous but only twenty-two at the time of Waterloo and could be a liability when in command. He had a 'minder' in the shape of Major General de Constant Rebecque – a Swiss national in Dutch service but of French Huguenot origin – who had followed him into exile, including a spell at Oxford, and whose contribution to the battle of Quatre Bras is often overlooked.

The Prince was wounded during the battle of Waterloo, and the Lion Monument marks the spot where it occurred.

Ensign Simpson: Ensign Charles Simpson, 2rd Battalion 3rd Guards, who entered the Regiment about three weeks after Tom. His family were landed gentry in Derby.[104]

His death is mentioned in a letter from Lieutenant Colonel Home to William Mudford, undated but probably written a year or two after the battle.[105] Simpson was wounded while lying down for shelter on the ridge, probably by a glancing cannonball. He was 'dreadfully lacerated' but 'remained perfectly sensible and aware of his situation', and died that evening after hours of horrible agony. Home was quite a senior officer, who took command inside Hougoumont when Macdonell was wounded, and Tom's statement that Simpson's death was universally regretted seems well borne out.

Lord Uxbridge: Lieutenant General Henry Paget, 2nd Earl of Uxbridge. He was Commander of the Anglo-Dutch Cavalry, who famously lost his leg during the final stages of the battle.

Uxbridge: 'By God, sir, I've lost my leg!'
Wellington: 'By God, sir, so you have!'

The tone of this exchange may have owed as much to relations between Wellington and Uxbridge as to British understatement. Uxbridge had deserted his own wife and eloped with the wife of Wellington's younger brother. Despite this, he was highly regarded as a cavalry commander and was forced upon Wellington as second-in-command. He survived the surgeons and lived until 1854.

'My friend Vane': This seems most likely to have been Ensign Henry Vane, 2/Coldstream Guards. He was commissioned about two months after Tom and it looks as if they shared a billet while stationed in Brussels.

On the day of Waterloo, the two senior officers of Vane's company were absent from Hougoumont: Lieutenant Colonel Sir William Gomm was on the staff and Lieutenant & Captain T.S. Cowell, who would have otherwise commanded the company, was taken sick on the day before. Responsibility therefore devolved on Vane, who had been commissioned only fifteen months earlier, and his fellow Ensign, The Hon. Walter Forbes. Forbes was about nine months younger than Tom and reputed to have been the youngest officer present at the battle.

Vane appears to have survived his wound as he features in the army list of 1818. *The Waterloo Roll Call* notes only that he was promoted Captain on 1 August 1822 and died at Sidmouth on 9 August 1829. His surname, or variants of it, is well known in aristocratic circles, but the author has been quite unable to find any more information about him.

APPENDIX III

THE STRUCTURE OF THE ANGLO-ALLIED ARMY

The Anglo-Allied army comprised two **Infantry Corps**, in theory each one about 25,000–30,000 strong, a **Cavalry Corps** about 15,000, and **Reserves** of about 34,000; some units of the Reserves were employed on garrison duty, so that the number of men available from the Reserves was reduced to about 19,000. Each formation contained troops from several different nations, although the proportions varied.

A Corps was intended to be a complete fighting unit – an idea copied from the French, as was the name. To the British it was, however, a rather new innovation and the structure was not quite as formal as it subsequently became; the cavalry and horse artillery remained a separate Corps, and the Reserves were under Wellington's direct command.

Below Corps level were the **Divisions**. Each allied force had its own divisional structures. In the case of the British, they were numbered by reference to the army as a whole, so that I Corps comprised the 1st and 3rd British Divisions; the 2nd and 4th British Divisions were in II Corps; and the 5th and 6th were in Reserve.

The British 1st and 6th Divisions each numbered just over 4,000 men, but the other British divisions were around the 7,000 mark. Tom was in the 1st (Guards) Division of I Corps, which comprised two **Brigades** of British infantry and the Divisional artillery of two batteries, one of which was provided by the King's German Legion (KGL).

Each brigade was made up of infantry **Battalions**, which can be slightly confusing; British infantry did not fight as whole regiments, but as individual battalions. Thus the 1st Division comprised the 2nd and 3rd Battalions of the 1st Foot Guards in the 1st Brigade, and the 2nd Battalions of the Coldstream and 3rd Foot Guards in the 2nd Brigade. The strength of battalions varied considerably. Those in the 1st Division were about 1,000 strong, and each brigade had only two battalions: by comparison the 3rd Division contained battalions of roughly half that size and a brigade in that division had correspondingly more battalions.

A battalion was in turn divided into **Companies**, and the structure is very clearly explained by Paget and Saunders.[106]

> *Each infantry battalion of the British Army consisted at full strength of six to ten companies, each up to 100 strong. One of them was a 'light company', which consisted of picked men trained as mobile troops and skirmishers, operating either as a company within their own battalion, or amalgamated to form a light battalion. Each battalion also had a 'grenadier company', again consisting of picked men. Originally the grenadiers were trained as assault troops, but by 1815 they were selected from the steadiest, most experienced men in a battalion.*

Tom's battalion comprised ten companies; he was in the 5th.

The defence of Hougoumont involved troops from four Divisions: the 1st, 2nd and 3rd British and the 2nd Netherlands Division. The 2nd and 3rd British Divisions were each about two-thirds German (KGL and Hanoverians). There were about 4,300 men in the numerically weak 1st British Division. The 2nd and 3rd British Divisions each contained about 8,000 men. The second Netherlands Division was about 7,600 strong.

Another source of confusion is the naming of the various regiments. They were basically known by a number which reflected their foundation, apart from the Coldstreams, who had been known by that name since 1670; in terms of age, they were the most senior regiment in the regular army but had missed out because of their Cromwellian origins. To make up for it, they adopted the motto *Nulli Secundus* and were never referred to – at least in their presence – as the 2nd Foot Guards.

Immediately after Waterloo the system began to give way to names that we would now recognise. The 1st Foot Guards became the Grenadiers, apparently on the basis that they had defeated the Grenadiers of the Imperial Guard; it appears that they had actually engaged the Chasseurs. A few years later Tom's regiment, the 3rd Foot Guards, became known as the Scots Fusilier Guards (to reflect their origins) and this was later shortened to the Scots Guards.

APPENDIX IV

BELGIAN UNITS IN THE ARMY OF THE UNITED NETHERLANDS

Tom's references to the Belgians bear examination. There were obviously understandable grounds for suspecting that some of them might not be entirely loyal to the Anglo-Allied cause, but it is fairly clear that Tom made only a hazy distinction between Dutch, Belgians and, for that matter, Germans. This was probably not helped by the army of the United Netherlands being a mixture of all three. The Belgian contingent at Waterloo was actually the smallest of them all – a little over 4,000 men, or 6% of the total.

Bijlandt's Brigade

There was one well-attested case in which a largely Dutch brigade retreated in disorder – or, as Tom puts it, ran away: and in this case, the Belgian element stood their ground. This has long been the cause of controversy, although the basic facts seem clear, and it may throw some light on the situation.

It occurred during the battle of Waterloo itself, and involved the 1st Brigade of the 2nd Netherlands Infantry Division, under Major General van Bijlandt. The Division itself was polyglot, comprising French-, Dutch- and German-speaking troops. The structure was reasonably logical, however, with the Dutch and Belgian regiments in the 1st Brigade, and Nassauers (actually German, but for dynastic reasons under Netherlands command) in the 2nd Brigade.

The Division had been the first to arrive at Quatre Bras, on the evening before the battle itself. The next day they fought well and incurred substantial losses; according to Adkin, the 1st Brigade had something under 3,000 men at Waterloo, at least 600 short of its original strength. Two regiments suffered particularly badly: the 5th Dutch Militia incurring 41% casualties and the 27th Dutch Jaegers dropping from over 800 to around 550 (i.e. more than 30%). On the evening of 16 June the Jaegers were sent to Nivelles to recover,[107] and appear to have been mistaken for Belgian deserters by Captain Mercer.[108] They re-joined the Anglo-Allied army in time for the actual Battle of Waterloo.

As we have already seen, Mercer was not averse to the odd scornful remark. His description of the event is so similar to Tom's that it seems likely that Tom was merely repeating what had then become common currency, rather than something that he witnessed for himself.

Accounts of what happened two days later at Waterloo, however, have provided one of the enduring debates about the battle. The traditional version is that for some unknown reason Bijlandt's Brigade – apart from the very much weakened 5th Dutch Militia, which was held in reserve – remained on the forward slope of the ridge, despite all the other formations taking up position on the reverse. The result was a terrible beating from artillery fire and apart from the 7th Belgian Line Regiment, which was possibly more experienced than the militia, they broke and retreated back through the Anglo-Allied lines.

As Adkin remarks, leaving them in front of the ridge as the only unit so exposed is difficult to believe, and is contradicted by other writers who had actually been present at the battle. However, it seems that they did retreat when they came under infantry attack; but after the losses that they had suffered, and bearing in mind their considerable inexperience, this is not altogether surprising.

Desertion rates

Unwillingness to confront the enemy is not quite the same as outright desertion, but Adkin's figures do however suggest that the Belgo-Dutch desertion rates were more than twice the average – and even more if the Duke of Cumberland's Hussars are treated as a special case and excluded from the calculation. This was a Hanoverian regiment made up of 'gentlemen amateurs', who witnessed the fall of La Haye Sainte, decided that they had had enough, and galloped back to Brussels.[109]

The British troops and the KGL were much more experienced and, perhaps surprisingly to modern eyes, well led. It is worth adding that the Prussian army – while less diverse – was by no means fully trained or well equipped, and that after the Battle of Ligny they too suffered badly from desertion.

APPENDIX V

BRITISH ARMY UNITS COMMITTED TO PORTUGAL

The most authoritative and complete source that lists the regiments involved is probably the *Naval & Military Magazine* for March 1827. Other sources exist, but in some cases these appear to be inaccurate and possibly reflect intentions that did not proceed.

The following details have been cross-checked against a series of detailed Regimental Histories that started to appear in the late 1830s. All but four of the officers are mentioned by name in Tom's Journal.

Divisional Commander   Lieutenant General Sir William Henry Clinton

Brigade level

Cavalry: Colonel Henry Wyndham

                        10th Hussars (two squadrons)
                        12th Lancers (two squadrons)

Guards Brigade: Major General Sir Henry Bouverie

                        1st Battalion Grenadiers
                        2nd Battalion Third Guards

1st Brigade: Major General Sir Edward Blakeney

                        4th Regiment
                        10th Regiment
                        23rd Regiment

2nd Brigade:	Major General Sir Thomas Arbuthnot
	11th Regiment
	43rd Regiment – *see below*
	63rd Regiment
Royal Artillery	Lieutenant Colonel Webber Smith (four batteries)
Royal Engineers	
Royal Staff Corps	One company
Royal Waggon Train	A detachment
Headquarters	Lieutenant Colonel Burgoyne
Staff	Colonel Sir E.M. McGregor – Deputy Adjutant-General
	Colonel Sir C.B. Vere, Bt, KCB – Deputy Quartermaster General
	Colonel R.G. Hare

The 43rd Regiment arrived in February 1827 and remained in Portugal for only six or seven months. It was probably sent when the situation looked critical and then withdrawn when the initial crisis was over, although this may have been influenced by the losses that they suffered from heatstroke during their return from Thomar.

Assuming the same sized battalions as the Grenadiers, this adds up to an initial force, excluding the 43rd but including Cavalry and others such as the Wagon Train, of roughly 5,000 men, which is consistent with most sources.

APPENDIX VI

SOURCES

Letters

The main starting point for information about Tom's involvement in the Battle of Waterloo – and indeed for family history during that period – is *A Century of Family Letters*, edited by Henrietta Litchfield, which contains three letters from Tom written just after the battle. There were actually two editions of this work: the first was privately published in 1904 and not intended for circulation outside the family. The second edition, of 1915, was for the general public and is about two-thirds the length; it sometimes omits material that is quite interesting, at least to a family historian.

In both editions it is clear that there are omissions in the second and third of Tom's letters – possibly for reasons of delicacy, as some of the content is quite graphic. The Wedgwood Museum holds the original of the first of these letters and full transcriptions of the other two, together with a number of other letters relevant to the campaign.

All of these are reproduced here. For reasons of clarity occasional corrections have been made to the punctuation and spelling.

Place names are more of a problem. The transcriptions vary in their versions of what is obviously the same place, possibly because of difficulty in deciphering Tom's handwriting – which is certainly not easy – and possibly because he was simply unfamiliar with local geography and language. The spelling of place names has also become more standardised since 1815, and versions that appear to have been generally accepted at the time have been substituted. In one or two cases the modern use of Flemish rather than French names can add a further complication, as maps do not always give both versions.

The letters can be found under the following references. Apart from the final letter, they are all in the Wedgwood Museum.

Date	Addressee	Comments	Reference
17 June 1815	Caroline Wedgwood	Transcription	W/M 1144/1
19 June 1815	Jenny Wedgwood	Original manuscript	W/M 31537-30
		Transcription	W/M 30.31537
24 June 1815	Jenny Wedgwood	Transcription (1)	W/M 1146/1
		Transcription (2)	W/M 1144/3
4 July 1815	Baugh Allen	Transcription	W/M E30 -31538.1 – 4
15 July 1815	John Wedgwood	Transcription	W/M 1144/2
14 Aug 1815	Baugh Allen	Transcription	W/M 1144/4
12 Mar 1835	William Siborne	Original manuscript	British Library Add Ms 34705, Fo 46

Portugal

Tom's Portuguese Journal was designed to keep his family up to date. It is basically a day-to-day record of events and experiences, although he often added his own views on what was going on and these can be quite revealing. He temporarily stopped keeping it on 14 August 1827, but resumed the practice – under family pressure – on 2 October 1827. The gap was filled with a long narrative summary.

A transcription of the entire Journal exists, and probably dates from about the same time as the later transcriptions of his Waterloo letters. A copy is held by the Wedgwood Museum.

Tom sent his Journal home in parts, at rather irregular intervals. The Wedgwood Museum has the original manuscript of the first part, covering the period from 30 December 1826 to 24 January 1827.

APPENDIX VII

BIBLIOGRAPHY

Adkin, Mark. *The Waterloo Companion,* Aurum Press, London (2001)

Audley, James A. *A Wedgwood at Waterloo,* The North Staffordshire Field Club Transactions and Annual Report for 1933–34

Burkhardt, Frederick and Smith, Sidney (ed). *The Correspondence of Charles Darwin, Vol 1*, Cambridge University Press (1985)

Chase, Malcolm. *1820 – Disorder and Stability in the United Kingdom,* Manchester University Press (2013)

Dalton, Charles. *The Waterloo Roll Call,* London (1890)

Davies, Margaret. *Victorian Naturalists in Tenby,* Tenby Museum and Art Gallery (1998)

Freemont-Barnes, Gregory. *Waterloo 1815,* The History Press (2014)

Glover, Gareth (ed). *The Waterloo Archive, Vol. I: British Sources,* Frontline Books, Yorkshire (2010)

Hamilton, Lieutenant General Sir F.W. *The Origin and History of the First or Grenadier Guards,* John Murray, London (1874)

Inglis-Jones, Elisabeth. *A Pembrokeshire County Family in the Eighteenth Century,* National Library of Wales Journal, XVII (1971), pp. 136-60, 217-37, 322-42

Kerry, Philip. *'He Fought at Waterloo': Thomas Josiah Wedgwood (1797–1860),* Journal of the Society for Army Historical Research, 82 (2004), pp. 191-203

Litchfield, H.E. *Emma Darwin: A Century of Family Letters,* privately printed, Cambridge University Press (1904)

Litchfield, H.E. *Emma Darwin: A Century of Family Letters,* John Murray, London (1915)

Livermore, H.V. *A New History of Portugal,* Cambridge University Press (1966)

MacKinnon, Colonel. *Origin and Services of the Coldstream Guards, Vol II*, London (1833)

Mercer, Cavalié. *Journal of the Waterloo Campaign*, William Blackwood (1870)

Miller, David. *The Duchess of Richmond's Ball*, Spellmount, Staplehurst (2005)

Muir, Rory. *Wellington – Waterloo and the Fortunes of Peace*, Yale (2015)

Robinson, Mike. *The Battle of Quatre Bras*, The History Press (2009)

Paget, Julian and Saunders, Derek. *Hougoumont – the Key to Victory at Waterloo*, Leo Cooper, London (1992)

Siborne, William. *The Waterloo Campaign 1815 (4th ed)*, Archibald Constable & Co, London (1895)

Stanhope, Philip Henry, 5th Earl. *Notes of Conversations with the Duke of Wellington, 1831–1851*, Longmans, Green New York (1888)

Summerville, Christopher. *Who was Who at Waterloo*, Pearson Education (2007)

Wedgwood, Barbara and Hensleigh. *The Wedgwood Circle, 1730–1897*, Collier Macmillan Canada (1980)

Wedgwood, Josiah C. *A History of the Wedgwood Family*, London (1908)

Wedgwood, Josiah C. and Joshua G.E. *Wedgwood Pedigrees*, Kendal (1925)

Wedgwood, Thomas Josiah. *Portuguese Journal*, unpublished

Windham-Quinn, Colonel. *Sir Charles Tyler, GCB, Admiral of the White*, London (1912)

ENDNOTES AND REFERENCES

In the case of published works, sources are generally given by reference to the surname of the author. For clarity and simplicity, exceptions have been made in certain cases, the main ones being:

CFL (1904)   *Emma Darwin: A Century of Family Letters* (1904 edition)

CFL (1915)   *Emma Darwin: A Century of Family Letters* (1915 edition)

Journal   Tom Wedgwood's Portuguese Journal

ENDNOTES

1 *CFL* (1915): Vol. I, p. 4. The 1904 edition goes into somewhat greater length about the Cresselly regime.

2 *CFL* (1904): Vol. I, p. 217.

3 *The Wedgwood Circle*: p. 192.

4 *The Record of Old Westminsters* implies that he spent only the Christmas term of 1811 at the school; this fits in with the *Sandhurst Archive Collection*, which lists 4 February [?] 1812 as his date of entry, leaving in 1813 – although the original document is in both cases very indistinct. The transcribed version of the Archive lists his Christian name as John; the original entry is indistinct, but the subject is clearly Tom, because his father is listed as John Wedgwood of Southend, which we know was where the family was living at the time. Subsequently, it appears from a letter in the *Wedgwood Archive Collection*, dated 11 January 1814, that a family friend, Edmund Currey, was prepared to arrange further private

tuition and encouragement in subjects relevant to his chosen profession. (*WAC 57/31542*)

5   Tom Wedgwood to his mother, 24 June 1815: 'My friend Vane, with whom I lived so long in Brussels....'

6   *Adkin*: p. 37. These figures are slightly higher than those in other accounts, but they are more coherent and the difference does not alter the overall point.

7   *The Wedgwood Circle*: p. 225.

8   *Mercer*: p. 212. Mercer eventually rose to the rank of General and his reminiscences, written-up from rough notes made during the campaign, were edited and printed by his son in 1870.

9   *The Wedgwood Circle*: p. 166; PS to Tom's letter to Baugh Allen of 4 July.

10   *Glover:* p. 138 – Letter 34.

11   *Adkin*: p. 336.

12   *Adkin*: p. 341.

13   *CFL* (1904): Vol. I, pp. 89-90.

14   *Stanhope*: p. 4.

15   *Steve Brown:* King George's Martinien at https://www.napoleon-series.org/military/organization/Britain/Casualties/KingGeorge/c_KingGeorge39.html

16   *CFL* (1904): Vol. I, p. 146 ff.

17   *Kerry*: p. 199.

18   *Gordon Taylor and Walls:* Sir Charles Bell (Edinburgh, 1958), p. 94. The authors, while mentioning figures of 146 primary and 225 secondary amputations (which figures seem rather low and are probably a subset) are careful not to ascribe these operations to Bell personally and then go on to say that 'in reality, he had only performed twelve amputations in all'! They do allow, however, that 'in the conservatism that he preached he was ahead of his time'.

19   *Sir Charles Bell – Obituary, The Gentleman's Magazine:* July–December

1842, pp. 99-100.

20 *Gordon Taylor and Walls:* Sir Charles Bell (Edinburgh, 1958), p. 94. The authors do not give the source of the figures, although they have been widely quoted elsewhere. They add that Bell himself complained that he could get little or no information about the result of his amputation cases after Waterloo.

21 *Adkin*: p. 312.

22 *CFL* (1904) pp. 53-4 is much more clear on this issue than the later one, which contains omissions. A letter from Jessie Allen, dated November 1813, implies that the Warden of Dulwich was supportive of Baugh's wish to marry.

23 *Lancelot Baugh Allen – Obituary, The Gentleman's Magazine*: January 1846, pp. 97-8.

24 *Journal of the Society for Army Historical Research*: Autumn 2004, Vol. 82, No. 331.

25 *MacKinnon*: p. 217. The author had fought at Hougoumont and wrote from first-hand experience.

26 *The Times*: 26 and 27 August 1819.

27 *Muir*: p. 142.

28 *Muir*: p. 159. *Croker Papers*, Vol. I: pp. 175-6. *The Times*: 17 June 1820.

29 *Journal*: 10 July 1827.

30 *Balfour, Charles B:* The Scots Guards (Glasgow, 1919), p. 31.

31 *Journal*: 6 and 14 February 1827.

32 *The Times*: 20 July 1822.

33 *Hansard*: 12 December 1826.

34 *Ross-of-Bladensburg, John:* A History of the Coldstream Guards from 1815 to 1895 (London, 1896), p. 75.

35 *The Times*: 14 December 1826.

36 *The Times*: 19 December 1826.

37 *The Times*: 22 December 1826.

38 *Journal*: 12 April 1827.

39 *Journal*: 18 June 1827.

40 *Journal*: 30 March 1827.

41 *Journal*: 2 January 1827.

42 *Journal*: 3 January 1827.

43 *Journal*: 29 March, 8 April 1827 and 20 March 1828.

44 *Childe Harold*: Canto I, Stanza XXV.

45 *Historical Record of the 4th Regiment of Foot*: p. 138.

46 The 12th Lancers seem to have more or less followed the infantry dispositions (*Historical Record of the 12th Lancers*: pp. 63-4); the *Historical Record of the 10th Royal Hussars* devotes a dozen short lines to their time in Portugal and says nothing about their actual involvement.

47 *Journal*: 31 January 1827.

48 *Journal*: 1 February 1827.

49 See, for example, the entries for 26 February, 3 and 5 March in Tom's *Journal*.

50 *Journal*: 20 June 1827.

51 *Journal*: 13 July 1827.

52 *Journal*: 21 March 1827.

53 *Journal*: 21 March 1827.

54 *The Regimental School System and Education in the British Army in the Napoleonic Era*: Haddaway. https://www.napoleon-series.org/military/organization/c_rgtschool1.html

55 *Annual Register for 1827*: p. 247 ff.

56 *Journal*: 11 March 1827.

57 *Historical Records of the 43rd Light Infantry*: p. 231, confirmed by Tom's *Journal* for 7 August 1827, which gives a figure of seven deaths and says that several others had gone 'raving mad'.

58 *Historical Record of the 11th Foot*: p. 83.

59 *Journal*: 9 August 1827 ff.

60 *The Sporting Magazine*: Vol. 21, 1 January 1828, pp. 222-4.

61   *Journal:* 27 May 1827.

62   *Journal:* 3 February 1828

63   *Journal:* 27 May 1827.

64   *Muir:* pp. 235-7.

65   Despite extensive searches, the author has been unable to find the original source of this story.

66   *Journal:* 25 February 1828.

67   *Livermore:* p. 270.

68   *Journal:* 27 March 1828.

69   *Journal:* 26 March 1828.

70   *Journal:* 24 March 1828.

71   *Journal:* 30 March 1828.

72   *Muir:* p. 314.

73   *The Correspondence of Charles Darwin:* Vol. 1, p. 283.

74   *CFL* (1904), Vol. 1: pp. 380.

75   *CFL* (1904), Vol. 1: pp. 380-81.

76   *The Wedgwood Circle:* p. 210.

77   *Boulston Marriage Register.*

78   Anne is stated to be 'of this Parish' in the *Boulston Marriage Register,* although for some reason the marriage was by licence rather than the calling of banns.

79   Portclew House, near the coast and a few miles southeast of Pembroke was occupied by Tom in 1838 (see *British Listed Buildings*). Portclew is also given as Tom's address in 1843, when he became a magistrate – see *ACCOUNTS & PAPERS Session 22 January–28 August 1846.*

80   *Wedgwood Pedigrees:* pp. 157-9.

81   *History of the Wedgwood Family:* p. 158.

82   This letter can be found only in the earlier, privately published, version of *A Century of Family Letters:* Vol. I, p. 459.

83   The *Clergy List* shows him as incumbent from 1832, when the church was built as a chapel of ease for St Chad's, Shrewsbury. Caroline Darwin

mentions him in a letter of 9 March 1834 – see *The Correspondence of Charles Darwin*: Vol. 1, p. 373.

84   *John Wedgwood of Bignall End*: Una des Fontaines, The Northern Ceramic Society Journal, Vol. V (1984).

85   See, for example, Ex Parte Gallimore in Rose, *Cases in Bankruptcy* (London, 1816), in which he attempted to get possession of a colliery which he had leased.

86   *CFL* (1904), Vol. 1: p. 459.

87   *Burke's* (1838).

88   They seem to have moved to St Mary's Hill, Tenby, in about 1844 – see *Coflein* Listing.

89   *CFL* (1904), Vol. 2: p. 133.

90   *CFL* (1904), Vol. 2: p. 134.

91   Kerry states that he appeared in 'three Commissions of the Peace held in 1838, 1844 and 1852'.

92   The *Tenby Observer*, 5 May 1870, 15 and 29 June 1855. It also lists him at various times as one of the 'The Resident Gentry' – and more importantly – gives his address.

93   *Davies*: p. 17 ff.

94   *The Wedgwood Circle*: p. 245, quoting from a letter from his sister Sarah. However, he seems to have spent at least some of the other winters in Tenby as well.

95   *CFL* (1904), Vol. 1: p. 240.

96   *Alumni Cantabridgienses to 1900*, Vol. 2. The *Clergy Lists* for that period do not mention this appointment, which may have been rather informal.

97   *CFL* (1904), Vol. 1: p. 283.

98   *CFL* (1904), Vol. 1: p. 216.

99   *Inglis-Jones*: p. 143.

100   *CFL* (1904), Vol. 1: p. 23.

101   *MacKinnon*: p. 221.

102   *History and Antiquities of Hengrave, Suffolk*: John Gage (1822), p. 78. *The Waterloo Roll Call* gives no biographical details for Thomas, and refers to Alexander as an only son, which must be incorrect.

103   *Miller*: p. 42.

104   *A Genealogical and Heraldic Dictionary of the Landed Gentry of Great Britain & Ireland*: Burke, London (1846).

105   *Glover*: *The Waterloo Archive – British Sources*, p. 142. Mudford wrote one of the earliest books on the 1815 campaign and this letter, now in the British Library, was probably part of his research.

106   *Paget and Saunders:* p. 27.

107   *Adkin*: p. 405.

108   *Mercer*: p. 250.

109   *Adkin*: pp. 37, 73 and 223.

PICTURE CREDITS